ABIDE in JESUS

Jesus' Command and
Our Opportunity

Dr. James M. Tarter

Abide in Jesus: a Special Fellowship in Him

I am amazed at how God has put a vital command right before our eyes in John 15:9, and about everyone has not seen it for what it is – including me for over 40 years. Jesus commanded: "abide (= stay) in My love." God is so loving and faithful to us in Jesus: how can I not stay in His love? When we see its meaning in Chapter 1, we can see that all of us should improve our staying in God's love to like Jesus stayed in it.

This book also fully addresses a second related problem. Standard translations of John's Gospel and 1John miss most of the emphasis on the special life and fellowship that God makes available to us in Jesus. This emphasis has been lost by an ambiguous translation of a simple Greek conjunction "*ina*" in about 10% of John's 213 *ina*'s. In a large majority of contexts, "that" or an infinitive fits John's use of *ina*, but "that" has many English meanings unlike John's use. With 25 *ina*'s, the context allows "that" or an infinitive to give an "apparent meaning" that differs from what I find for all of John's *ina*'s (telic: projecting to an end, outcome, or purposeful goal). We shall see that "*ina* = so that" for these 25 *ina*'s (in contrast to the shortened "that" 24 times in the KJV and 23 times in the NAS) brings out this missing emphasis (or content).

How does this "little" translation issue impact John 15:9's "abide in My love" and 15:4's "abide in Jesus"? In an amazing way that we shall see, translating these 25 *ina*'s as the full "so that" reveals that "abide in Jesus" is a key theme in all of John's Gospel and 1John, and normally should be a part of the foundation for a believer's life on earth.

Part 1 (Chapters 1-6) shows the major new content opened up by fully translating *ina* each time John used it. Part 1 essentially duplicates a shorter book, *Stay in My Love*, which shows the major missed content without the Part 2 examination. Chapter 7 can help readers draw a firmer conclusion about God's and John's true meaning of *ina*: its usually assumed meanings, or its meaning in this book that fits all of John's *ina*'s and opens up a key theme in his Gospel and 1John. Chapter 8 shows a telic source-outcome meaning for each of John's 213 *ina*'s.

CONTENTS

Abide in Jesus

Jesus' Command and Our Opportunity

Part 1: A Vital Unseen Theme in John's Gospel and 1John

1. Our Life in Jesus Shown in John 15:4-10 5

2. A Telic *Ina* Shows Jesus' and Our Food 11

3. Jesus' New Commandment in John 13-15 21

4. Jesus' Telic Praying in John 17 29

5. The John 15 Fellowship in All 1John 35

6. Spiritually Informative Verses in 1-2John 43

Part 2: What Is God's and John's True Meaning of *Ina*?

7. John's *Ina* and John's *Oti* 55

8. How Each of John's *Ina*'s Can Be Telic 73

Appendices

1. Complete Groups of *Ina*-Verses 99

2. All of John's *Oti*-Verses 115

3. Comparing Entire Groups of John's *Ina*- and *Oti*-Verses .. 127

About the Author 147

DEDICATION

to

MY WONDERFUL WIFE NITA

Whose fellowship and life with God in Jesus
has produced His love in her life

ISBN: 978-1-79482-994-7

Unless noted otherwise, Scripture taken from the NEW AMERICAN STANDARD BIBLE® (1995 Updated Edition): © 1960, 1962, 1963, 1968, 1971, 1972, 1973, 1975, 1977, 1995 by the Lockman Foundation. Used by permission. (www.Lockman.org)

I call the New American Standard Bible the NAS. I add boldface, underlining, and capitals to specific words and phrases in Scriptures in order to add my emphasis for discussion. I also occasionally call parts of verses "a" or "b".

A quote of Alfred Marshall on p. 17 is taken from *The Interlinear NASB-NIV Parallel New Testament in Greek and English*, copyright © 1993 by Zondervan Publishing House. Used by permission of Zondervan. www.zondervan.com

A comparison of two Greek words for "know" and for "ask" is taken from *Vine's Complete Expository Dictionary of Old and New Testament Words*, W. E. Vine, Thomas Nelson Publishers, 1996.

Quotes about the Greek Subjunctive, Indicative, and Imperative moods on p. 56 and 108 are taken from the Grammatical Notations in the *Hebrew-Greek Key Word Study Bible*, Spiros Zodhiates, AMG Publishers, 2008.

Eighth edition, 2020

Chapter 1

Our Life in Jesus Shown in John 15:4-10

Abide in Me and abiding in the Vine in John 15:1-11 are well-known Scriptures. Two key features about v. 1-11 are normally not realized or seen. One is God's call and our opportunity shown in v. 4-10: to <u>stay</u> in a life and fellowship with Father God, Son Jesus, and other believers in Him, which He compared to His life and fellowship with His Father. The second feature is to see that this truly is a theme in John's Gospel.

Let us see more exactly what I have just declared. In Chapter 1 we see this theme that is rarely seen in John 15:9-10. In Chapters 2-6 we see how other well-known verses in John's Gospel, 1John, and 2John connect to this theme. In Chapters 2 and 7 we can see the <u>systematic reason</u> why normally we do not see this theme.

Consider what Jesus said in John 15:4a and 15:9-10:

[4]***Abide in Me, and I in you***.... (John 15:4a)

[9]*Just <u>as</u> My Father has loved Me, I have also loved you;* ***ABIDE IN MY LOVE***. [10]***IF*** *you* ***keep My commandments***, ***you will abide in My love****; just* ***as I have kept*** *My Father's commandments and* ***abide in His love***." (John 15:9-10)

You see the command in v. 4 and the capitalized command in v. 9. <u>Abide</u> means to <u>stay</u>, <u>remain</u>, or continue. V. 9 could seem like God's easiest command to obey, but v. 10 shows a very <u>different key content</u> of v. 9 than <u>not</u> <u>disobeying</u> Jesus' command. "Stay [abide] in My love" must <u>NOT be CONFUSED</u> with great truths of <u>God's faithful love</u> in Jesus to all believers and <u>His always being with us</u>. Here are two of the many Scriptures stating <u>these other</u> two great truths:

*For I am convinced that **neither...nor any other created thing**, will be **able to separate us from the love of God**, which is in Christ Jesus our Lord.* (Rom. 8:38-39)

*...**I am with you always**, even to the end of the age.* (Matt. 28:20)

John 15:9 commands us disciples, "stay in His love". We often add ideas of how I can disobey, or the consequence (penalty) if I disobey. But v. 10 shows that these ideas are not the heart of this command: "*¹⁰**IF** you **keep My commandments**, **you will abide in My love**; just **AS I have kept** My Father's commandments and **abide in His love**.*" All who have not always lived like perfectly obedient Jesus lived on earth have already experienced what it means to not abide in His love. We do not need to learn how we have lived, but learn God's way to live better, and v. 9-10 reveal that He has made it available.

In both v. 10 and v. 9, Jesus says "just as" in comparing His and our FULFILLING v. 9's command to abide in His love. Consider that the Father's love for and staying with Jesus would not have stopped IF He did not keep a command, but keeping all His Father's commands was a key part of Jesus' "abiding in His love". V. 9-10 show our OPPORTUNITY and CALLING to stay in this FELLOWSHIP like Jesus had with His Father while on earth, and Jesus calls this abiding life and fellowship "staying in My love". This command seems to be so easy to fulfill, but this fellowship is so special that nearly all believers (including me) lack much evidence of truly staying in His love like Jesus did.

Jesus' *"abide in Me, and I in you"* command in John 15:4 (p. 5) is really another way to say the same command in v. 9-10: to stay in this special fellowship in Jesus. 1John 1 uses this term "fellowship" 4 times to represent THIS LIFE IN JESUS, and 1John 2:6 identifies another key revealing feature of this life of staying (= abiding) in Jesus:

*the one who says **he abides in Him** [Jesus, God] ought himself to **walk** in the **same manner** as He walked.* (1John 2:6)

Then how did Jesus walk? Consider John 5:19 and 30:

*Truly, truly, I say to you, the **Son can do <u>nothing</u> of Himself**, **unless** it is something **He sees the Father** doing; for whatever the Father does, these things the **Son also does in like manner**.* (Jesus in John 5:19)

*I can do **<u>nothing</u> on My own initiative**. **As I hear, I judge**; and My judgment is just, because **I do not seek My own will**, but **the will of Him who sent Me**.* (Jesus in John 5:30)

As a foundational feature of living like Jesus on earth, He <u>did only</u> what He saw and heard His invisible Father do and say: <u>ALL JESUS DID AND SAID</u> in His life on earth <u>came from His Father</u>. Jesus adds in John 14:10: "*...The words that I say to you <u>I do **not speak** on My own initiative</u>, but <u>the **FATHER ABIDING IN ME** does His works</u>.*"

Jesus quotes a Scripture (Deut. 8:3) <u>for Himself and mankind</u> in the first wilderness temptation in Matt. 4:4: "**<u>Man shall not live</u>** on <u>bread alone</u>, **but** on **<u>every word</u>** that **proceeds out of the <u>mouth of God</u>**." <u>Jesus ate and we eat</u> and digest <u>what God says to us</u>. As Jesus our Example showed in the Matt. 4 temptations, He heard God's words and they came out in what Jesus did. Therefore <u>we</u> should <u>hear</u> and <u>eat</u> <u>what God says to us</u>, and we <u>should let it come out in what we do</u>.

John 6:56-57 shows more about <u>our</u> eating and <u>abiding in Jesus</u>:

[56]*He who **EATS My flesh** and drinks My blood **ABIDES in Me, and I in him**.* [57]***AS** the living Father sent Me, and **I LIVE** **because of the Father,** <u>so</u> he who **eats Me**, he also <u>will **live** because of Me</u>.*

What a profound word by Jesus! *"I live because of the Father"* is a part of <u>an analogy</u> in which the one who eats Jesus *"will <u>live because of Me</u>"* and *"<u>abides in Me, and I in him</u>"* [the believer]. As we are seeing, <u>everything</u> Jesus <u>did</u> came from <u>His abiding fellowship with His Father</u>, in which <u>Jesus saw and heard God's judgments</u> of what to do and how to do it. And <u>Matt. 4:4 draws an analogy</u> of this <u>hearing and doing His words</u> to <u>eating them like eating bread</u>. This analogy is taken much further in John 4-6, as we shall see in Chapter 2 (p. 12-17).

Now consider *"Abide in Me and I in you"* (John 15:4) and John 15:7:

[7]**IF <u>you abide in Me</u>**, *and* **<u>My words abide in you</u>**, **ask whatever you wish**, *and it will be* **done for you**. [8]*My Father is glorified by this, that* **you bear much fruit**, *and so prove to be My disciples.* (John 15:7-8)

Here we focus on what all of this abiding (= staying) shows about <u>our</u> life-giving <u>fellowship</u> with Father God and Jesus. He <u>did</u> <u>only</u> what His Father did and wanted, and <u>so</u> He <u>asked</u> accordingly. Therefore "<u>abide</u> <u>in Jesus</u>" includes <u>asking as He would ask</u>, and <u>asking for</u> <u>anything else</u> is <u>not</u> "as He walked" and not abiding in Him (1John 2:6 on p. 6). My desire to <u>hear and obey God's words</u> to me like Jesus did will cause me to ask like Him and <u>receive His instruction if I am not</u>. Therefore <u>I need</u> to <u>stay in close fellowship with God</u>: it <u>produces the</u> <u>fruitful life like Jesus lived</u> that the end of v. 7 and v. 8 describe.

Unlike Jesus, I have often not heard nor seen what my heavenly Father is saying or doing. As we shall see when we get to 1John 1:9-2:2 (Chapter 6), this is precisely the context for the great promise: if we confess our sins (here a <u>sin</u> is <u>missing the mark</u> of <u>hearing and doing</u> <u>whatever</u> He <u>truly says to us</u>), then He is faithful and just to forgive us our sins and cleanse us from all unrighteousness. He fully restores us justly into the <u>special fellowship</u> that God provides for us <u>only in Jesus</u> (which is described in John 15:4-17 and 1John).

I also need to <u>let Jesus' words</u> <u>abide in me</u>. Either I let His words keep working throughout my whole heart and life, or else I keep them out of some part. If I let them abide in me, then they will direct me and change my self-seeking nature: they will <u>transform my heart</u>. This will shape "whatever I wish" – whatever my heart chooses. If I ask for anything outside of His will, then His words will correct me. I let His words produce their Godly results in me, or else I shall find ways to remove His words, to not let them stay in me. This part of the promise in John 15:7 tells me to <u>let Him change my heart</u> <u>into</u> <u>desiring His will</u>.

For example, I can wish and ask Almighty God for $1,000,000 now to meet a friend's urgent need. I ask for this solution with my limited knowledge and wisdom, but I keep asking for and listening for God's wisdom. In this situation, He might tell me to love him in specific ways without giving this money through me. God may want to address this need in ways that provide for my friend's eternal development, while my way puts me in the center and might work against the best long-term good for both him and me. If I insist on my initial solution, then I am not letting God's words stay in me to change my heart and mind.

We have seen highlights from John 15:4-10 that reveal a <u>very special abiding fellowship</u>. I emphasize that relationship and <u>fellowship</u> are different: to illustrate, a 2-year-old's temper tantrum or defiance disrupts his fellowship with his good parent until the child changes to get back on track, but does not disturb their secure, loving relationship.

Consider John 15:6a: *"If anyone does <u>not abide in Me</u>, he is thrown away as a branch and dries up."* This is not tossing a relationship, but is <u>drying up</u> this <u>very special fellowship in Jesus</u> described in John 15:1-17 and 1John, and is <u>losing usefulness</u> for glorifying God (15:7-8) and for producing fruit (15:8). 15:6 is "one thing" Jesus spoke about in 15:11: *"<u>These things</u> I have **spoken to you so that** My joy may be in you, and that **your joy** may be **full**."* V. 6 is not joyful <u>if</u> it tells us our <u>relationship</u> with God is so fragile. As p. 6 emphasizes, *"abide in My love"* reveals an <u>opportunity for this fellowship with God</u>, not a limit to His love. But <u>sin</u> can disrupt this fellowship (1John 3:5-8, p. 45): <u>God and His words abiding in us give us His power to abide in Him</u>.

How Being Born Again Fits into the Theme of This Special Fellowship

There is more to see about this fellowship in v. 4-10, even more in 15:1-17, still more in John's whole Gospel, and still more in 1John. As we shall see later, here is a fuller expression of this <u>theme</u> in John's Gospel: <u>first</u> we <u>truly connect</u> to (<u>fully receive</u>) <u>Father God through His</u>

Son Jesus, and then we stay in the special fellowship with God that Jesus compares to what He had with His Father while on earth. This fellowship will produce needed vital outcomes, such as all of our works in God, increased believing in Jesus, and loving others better by His loving Spirit. In order to start seeing how this special fellowship is a vital theme of John's whole Gospel, let us see key verses in John 1-3 about how we get started in our special fellowship with God.

> *But as many as **received Him** [Jesus], to them **He gave** the right to **become children of God**, even to those who **believe in His name**.* (John 1:12)
>
> *Do not be amazed that I said to you, "You **must be born again**."* (Jesus in John 3:7)

John 1:12 shows how we get the right to become God's child: to receive Jesus, which is the "truly connect to the true God through Jesus" that is the first part of this theme in John's Gospel (John 6:45, 6:53-54, 8:47, 10:1-7, 14:6). Then John 3 shows a needed first step in becoming His child: being born again is also in the first part of this theme. Notice a child's role in this stage of forming a relationship with his/her father: nothing to do with the conception (like John 6:44 and 15:16), and fully receiving or embracing the father's initiatives to bond (John 1:12). After this relationship is established, the child will have an increasing role in maintaining the fellowship or reconnecting if needed.

More to See About Our Opportunity to Live in This Fellowship

Chapters 2-6 show many verses related to Jesus' command for us to get in and then stay in this life in Him. It is a vital theme in the whole Gospel of John, and was a key part of the foundation of the anticipated initial 1John receivers. (I clarify: those who were not in this fellowship were relating to those who were in it). We shall see one unintentional mistake that has hindered centuries of believers from fixing their SOURCE problem (not staying in Jesus' love, not staying in Him) so that they could better move into vital long-term OUTCOMES.

Chapter 2

A Telic Ina Shows Jesus' and Our Food

In Chapter 1 we saw how Jesus' command to "stay in Him" and to "stay in His love" actually reveals our great opportunity to live our lives with Father God like Jesus lived with Him while on earth. We also saw (p. 6) how *"abide in My love"* was hidden right in front of our eyes for hundreds of years (including my eyes for decades after knowing John 15 well), and yet this insight was there for us to see and embrace the whole time. A second problem veils what John shows us about his Gospel's theme of <u>living in fellowship with God like Jesus did</u>. This time the problem is not in what we overlook (unless we know Greek well), but the veil is provided by <u>not</u> <u>fully</u> translating the word *ina* about 10% of the 213 times John used it. <u>John's use shows us what he means</u>.

In Chapter 2 we shall briefly discuss translations of *ina* with its impact on the veiled theme illustrated in two key verses (John 4:34, 6:29). In Chapters 3-4 we shall see how fully translating *ina* in the other 11 key *ina*-verses in John's Gospel impacts this theme.

The Key to Seeing John's Theme Clearly: Rightly Translate Ina

<u>Consistently</u> translating 22 well-known verses with the way John used all 213 of his *ina*'s reveals a simple but vital <u>theme</u> in John's Gospel and 1John that we normally do not read in English.

Ina is a Greek conjunction that John used in the form "A *ina* B" to <u>connect</u> <u>a source or start A</u> with <u>its projected or possible outcome B</u>. These *ina*'s are usually translated compatible with a meaning like "<u>so</u> <u>that</u>", "in order that", "in order to", "with the result that", or "for the purpose of", and usually this is simplified to "that" or "to". But "that" or "to" can lose *ina*'s primary force to connect a source with a projected outcome or end if a "source or start A" contains a word(s) that needs to be rightly identified (examples are "this", "new commandment", or "My food"). In 22 English verses, we naturally read B as identifying A instead of being a projected outcome or end of A. It is so natural that I should explain each *ina*-Scripture as I introduce it. We begin by seeing that Jesus' true food equipped Him to do His works, which were an OUTCOME of what He ate: what He ate was a SOURCE of His works.

John 4:34 – Jesus' and Our Food, and Its Outcome: His and Our Works

Both before and after my wife Nita and I learned about the *ina* in John 4:34, it was a favorite verse of ours. A consistent *ina* has revolutionized v. 34 for us, but only to give us a better perspective and to see how this Scripture connects to John 15. Consider John 4:32-34:

> ..."I have **food to eat** that **you do not know about**." [33]So the disciples were saying to one another, "No one brought Him anything to eat, did they?" [34]Jesus said to them, "**My food** is **to [ina] do** the will of Him who sent Me and to accomplish His work." (John 4:32-34)

In v. 32 Jesus says that His disciples did not know about His food, and in v. 34 He connects His food to what He did. No food is identified in the close context of v. 34. The usual translation of v. 34's *ina* ("to") plainly says that Jesus' food was to do His Father's will and to accomplish His work. In contrast, *ina*'s consistent meaning in v. 32-34 shows that Jesus ate UNIDENTIFIED FOOD in order to produce 4:34's stated outcome: Jesus' DOING and accomplishing His Father's will and work. If this is true, then what was Jesus' food?

A far larger context of v. 34, John 4:32-15:17 and especially 4:32-6:57, shows the TRUE FOOD for Jesus and also for believers in Him. We saw and discussed eating God's words in Chapter 1. Remember:

*[19]Truly, truly, I say to you, the **Son can do nothing** of Himself, **unless** it is something **He sees the Father** doing; for whatever the Father does, these things the **Son also does** in like manner....[30]I can **do nothing** on My own initiative. **As I hear, I judge**; and My judgment is just, because **I do not seek My own will**, but **the will of Him who sent Me**.* (John 5:19, 30)

*[51]I am the **living bread** that came down out of heaven; if anyone **eats** of this bread, he will **live forever**; and the **bread** also **which I WILL GIVE** for the life of the world **is My flesh**....[55]For **My flesh is TRUE FOOD**, and **My blood is true drink**. [56]He who **EATS My flesh** and drinks My blood **ABIDES in Me, and I in him**. [57]**AS** the living Father sent Me, and **I live because of the Father,** so he who eats Me, he also will **live** because of Me.* (John 6:51, 55-57)

*[10]...[b]The words that I say to you I do not speak on My own initiative, but the **Father abiding in Me does His works**. [11]Believe Me that **I am in the Father** and the **Father is in Me**; [b]....[20]In that day you **will know** that **I am in My Father**, and **you in Me**, and **I in you**.... [15:4]Abide in Me, and I in you.... [9]Just **AS** My Father has loved Me, I have also loved you; **abide in My love**. [10]IF you **keep My commandments**, you will abide in My love; just **AS I have kept** My Father's commandments and **abide in His love**."* (John 14:10b-11a, 20 and 15:4a, 9-10)

John 5:19 and 30 show clearly that Jesus did only what He saw and heard from His Father: ALL Jesus DID came from His Father. Jesus' comparison in John 6:56-57 calls this kind of source "eating". Jesus ate special food in His special fellowship with His Father: in it Jesus heard and saw His work to do. He ate HIS TRUE FOOD in order to EQUIP Him to DO His Father's will and work, the stated OUTCOME in John 4:34. The disciples did not know Jesus' true food in 4:32-34, but kept learning about it until He made it explicit in John 15.

John 6:57 shows Jesus the Man living because of His Father. John 15:4-10 with 14:10b-11a, 20 commands us to stay in a special unity and fellowship like Theirs. In it we eat our true food – His flesh – and this equips us to stay in Him (6:55-56). In this special fellowship, we eat and live on every word He says to us: *"**Man shall not LIVE** on bread alone, but on every word that proceeds out of the mouth of God"*

(Matt. 4:4, Deut. 8:3). Our true food is Jesus with all He tells us (our *Logos*), and we eat it to live our eternal life. As we eat our true food He gives us (John 6:51, above) and let it come out in our actions and lives, we abide (stay) in Jesus and in His love. In order to eat our true food from Jesus, we first receive (truly connect to) Jesus (John 1:12, p. 10).

John 15 shifts our focus from what we eat in our fellowship to this special fellowship with God in which we eat this true food. We stay in the Vine (v. 1-6); we stay in Him with Him in us (v. 4); and we stay in His love as He stayed In His Father's love (v. 9). This abiding is a life with Him like Jesus had with Him and provides ample opportunity for us to eat true food like He did. We eat what we hear from Him, and can do what He tells us as He kept His Father's commandments. V. 9-10 (and 15:14, 1John 1:9-2:2, 2:3-6, p. 43-44) show that keeping His commands is a key way to check and know that we are staying in His love. (As "my Lord", anything He tells me to do is His command to me).

In John 6:27 Jesus commands those following Him to WORK FOR THE FOOD (our *Logos* or Word) that HE WILL GIVE THEM:

[27]Do not **WORK** for the food which perishes, but **FOR THE FOOD** which **endures to ETERNAL LIFE**, which **the SON OF MAN WILL GIVE TO YOU**, for on Him the Father, God, has set His seal." (John 6:27)

The Scriptures we considered so far can help us realize that we eat this true food Jesus gives for eternal life (John 6:27, 51-57) as we stay in Jesus – stay in this fellowship with God that Jesus compares to His fellowship or life with His Father while on earth. What is this work for life? Jesus' key command in v. 27 to all following Him has usually been lost to English readers by translations of *ina* as "that" or "to" in John 6:29. Let us see John 6:27-29 in its larger and smaller contexts.

John 6:26-58 – Believe in Jesus: Our Work from God? Or Its Outcome?

In John 4-15, Jesus said in 4:32 that He had food to eat that His disciples did not know about, and the "consistent meaning" of *ina* in 4:34 shows that His food, unidentified near John 4:32-34, is a SOURCE of this end or OUTCOME: all that He did. In John 5:19, 30 Jesus tells us that He can do nothing unless He sees or hears it from His Father. In John 15:4-10 Jesus commands us disciples to abide in our special fellowship with God in Jesus that is like His was with His Father. John 6:55-57 explicitly connects our eating the true food – *Logos* Jesus with all He tells us – to our abiding life in Him: we get into it and stay there.

In John 6:1-25 Jesus had fed the 5000 and walked on water. The multitude following Him in v. 26-58 saw signs (healings, v. 2), were in a great sign (v. 14), and noticed His amazing ability to escape everyone when they sought Him (v. 22-26), so that Jesus had given them many fresh signs. This is v. 27-29's small context: in it Jesus identified the work of God that He tells us to do (we who would follow Him):

> [26]*Jesus answered them and said, "Truly, truly, I say to you, you* **seek** *Me, not because you saw signs, but* **because you** *ate of the loaves and were* **filled**. [27]*Do not* **WORK** *for the food which perishes, but* **FOR THE FOOD** *which* **endures to eternal life**, *which* **the Son of Man will GIVE TO YOU**, *for on Him the Father, God, has set His seal."* [28]*Therefore they said to Him, "What shall we do, so that [ina] we may* work the works of God?" [29]*Jesus answered and said to them,* **"This** *is the* **work of God**, *that [ina] you believe in Him whom He has sent." *[30]**So** *they said to Him, "What then* **do You do for a sign**, *so that [ina] we may see, and believe You? What* **work do You perform?"** (John 6:26-30, and notice especially v. 27)

We see again Jesus' command to His followers in v. 27: "**work**...**for** the **food**...the **Son** of Man will **give to you**." This WORK for THIS FOOD is to stay in our special fellowship with God after first truly connecting to Him: do what we need to KEEP RECEIVING Him! In v. 28 Jesus' followers asked what they could do to work the works of God. Jesus already told them His answer in His command in v. 27: work for the RIGHT FOOD – "**This**" as He began His answer in v. 29!

In the way John consistently used *ina* (you see it in v. 28, 30), v. 29's bold *ina* shows that v. 27's work for the TRUE food from Jesus (truly receive God) is the work of God for His followers, and receiving Him leads to this OUTCOME: they believe in Jesus. Here is a telic *ina* translation of v. 29's answer: *"**This** [v. 27] is the **work of God**, **SO THAT** you may **believe into Him** whom He has sent."* Our special fellowship with Jesus provides a vital way to increase believing in Him: we who have lived in this fellowship and life can confirm that it does.

In contrast, every English translation of v. 29 that I see agrees with "the work of God for His followers IS 'to believe in Jesus'". With A - B symbols identified on p. 11, this translates *ina* B [= believe in Jesus] AS IF it identifies the work of God (A): identifying "believing" as God's work for us is a very different meaning of this vital "Spiritually-Informative *ina*-Verse" (SIV).

John 6 after v. 29 confirms the consistent meaning of *ina* in v. 29. In v. 30 Jesus' followers asked for a sign so that they could see it and believe Jesus. Their request really was a lie, and Jesus did not answer it like a true request. As we saw (p. 15), in 6:1-26 they saw healings, were in two more signs, and were following Him because one sign satisfied their appetite: they were seeking to be filled more than a sign.

In fact, in John 6:45 Jesus shows that NO SIGN would help their unbelief: *"...**Everyone** who has heard and learned **from the Father, comes to Me**."* The context shows clearly that they had followed Jesus but did NOT COME TO HIM like 6:45 says: they did NOT TRULY CONNECT to Father God and had NO HUNGER to connect, so that they COULD NOT BELIEVE. In v. 28 they asked for work that Jesus had already told them in v. 27, and in v. 30 asked for a sign to believe Him while refusing a great sign (feeding the 5000: them!). They failed to connect because they DENIED the SOURCE of their problem: they

were <u>NOT truly</u> connected to God <u>and did NOT WANT</u> to connect –
they were <u>refusing to receive</u> <u>Him</u> or <u>His work</u> (this theme in John).

They did need to move into 6:29's <u>OUTCOME</u> of believing in Jesus:
*"Truly, truly, I say to you, he who **believes has eternal life**"* (John
6:47). Believing a lie can be deadly, and <u>believing in Jesus</u> is the way
to <u>lay hold of eternal life</u>: our need to believe in Him is <u>not reduced by a</u>
<u>consistent *ina*</u>. This *ina* does uncover this buried treasure for us in John
6 and helps us to <u>move better into God's ways</u>: <u>if I continually do not</u>
<u>effectively</u> believe in Jesus, then <u>I need</u> to <u>RECEIVE HIM</u> – <u>TRULY</u>
<u>CONNECT OR RE-CONNECT TO GOD IN JESUS</u> instead of <u>trying</u>
<u>harder to believe</u> in Him. Many in the Church have shown clearly for
nearly 2000 years how to truly connect with Him, so that in this book we
move into discussing the key issue about *ina* instead of that vital topic.

John's Meaning of Ina: Consistently <u>Telic</u>? Or Ina May Be Like Oti?

So far you have seen four examples of the way John's *ina* has
normally been translated into English: "so that" in John 6:28, 30, "to" in
4:34, and "that" in 6:29. You have also seen that "so that" in John 4:34
and 6:29 brings out a remarkably different (but Bible-consistent)
practical meaning to both of these vitally important, informative verses.
These examples provide a good foundation for further discussing *ina*.

In Marshall's Introduction to his *Interlinear Greek-English New
Testament* (on p. xiii, 1993 Edition), he makes a remarkable statement
about the use of "*ina*" in the New Testament (I add underlining):

> Strictly speaking, <u>*ina*</u> is a "<u>telic</u>" particle – that is, it denotes <u>purpose</u>
> (<u>*telos*</u>, "an <u>end</u>"); hence a <u>full translation</u> is "<u>in order that</u>". But
> inasmuch as in New Testament times there was a tendency to use it
> where <u>*oti*</u> would be expected, it <u>sometimes means no more</u> than the
> <u>conjunction</u> "<u>that</u>" (e.g., Matt. 5:29).

Bible translations make Marshall's last half-sentence an <u>assumed</u>
"fact", not a mere personal conclusion.

Matt. 5:29 is the fourth out of about 700 times *ina* is used in the New Testament, and looks like the first very clear example in which *ina* was used where *oti* SEEMED to be expected. But as I saw how <u>John</u> used *ina* 213 times and *oti* 413 times, and how every translation (that I have seen) translated well-known spiritually-informative verses (SIV's), I found stunning results.

Ina in John could <u>consistently</u> lead to or project toward an <u>END or OUTCOME</u>. In contrast, *oti* further identified what came "before" *oti* in 57% of John's uses and showed why (because) 43% of them. I also found that God through John carefully and distinctly used *ina* and *oti*. But <u>if a word in *ina*'s antecedent</u> is <u>not clear</u>, translators often treat *ina* as if it were *oti*, so that we English readers would <u>not realize *ina*'s telic meaning</u> and even have it <u>unintentionally</u> veiled from us: as Marshall inferred, "that" (from *oti*) is <u>often not telic in English</u> (neither is "to" when it is an infinitive like "to do" in John 4:34 on p. 12-14).

John's *ina* and *oti* are conjunctions usually in the form A *ina* B and A *oti* B, where statement part A is before *ina* or *oti*, and part B is after *ina* or *oti*. In 210 of 213 *ina*'s, I find that <u>*ina*</u> shows <u>A might somehow lead to, cause, precede, produce, set up, or result in what B shows</u> (an <u>OUTCOME</u>); the other 3 of 213 are "telic-extents". This <u>source A – outcome B relationship</u> can be called <u>TELIC</u> from the Greek word *telos*, which shows an end or limiting extent, outcome ... (more in the {note} below). Words to express a TELIC *INA* include <u>SO THAT</u>, <u>IN ORDER THAT</u>, IN ORDER TO, WITH A RESULT THAT, and FOR THE PURPOSE OF. A shortened "that" is ambiguous, with a telic meaning <u>in some contexts</u> <u>but not others</u>: "that" has <u>many non-telic uses in English</u> and does <u>not by itself</u> <u>suggest</u> a telic meaning.

{ A note to translators. Some may restrict "telic" to show only purpose, but I consider the Biblical use of *telos* and find it used to express an <u>end</u> or limiting extent, <u>outcome</u>, fulfillment, purpose, or termination. Matt. 26:58, Rom. 6:21-

22, 2Cor. 11:15, Heb. 6:11, James 5:11, and 1Peter 1:9 show fulfilling outcomes not restricted to purpose. I find that "source-outcome" very well fits John's use of *ina* and can fit well into the Bible's actual use of *telos* ("telic"). }

With John often using the form "A *ina* B" to connect a source or start A to its projected or possible outcome B, I often write this telic sequential relationship as A → B. *Ina* normally implies an order with A and B: a projected outcome or extent (end) B must have a source or start A. Telic-extents are a figurative A → B that also needs a good A. Here are examples of his 210 *ina* telic-outcomes and 3 *ina* telic-extents (each ***ina*** is in **bold**).

John 1:7: *He came as a witness, **to** testify about the Light, **so that** all might believe through him.* The first *ina* shows "John's coming as a witness" to be a source A for a projected outcome: testifying about the Light (literally, "as a witness so that he could testify about the Light" – testifying is an action that a witness may do). Testify about the Light is the second *ina*'s source A, and A's projected or desired outcome B was for all to believe through him. *Ina*'s A → B twice

John 1:22: *...Who are you, **so that** we may give an answer to those who sent us?...* Their asking Jesus, "Who are you?" (A), was the source for this intended outcome B: they could give an answer to their senders. As always, a specified A may be part of a larger A (their previous questions) or may not be B's only source. *Ina*'s A → B

Rev. 13:13: *He performs great signs, **so that** he even makes fire come down out of heaven to the earth in the presence of men.* *Ina* B is strictly not a "sequential outcome" of A, but shows how far A (great signs) may extend. Therefore *ina* retains its telic meaning: B shows how far figuratively great signs (A) may go (A → B). John 1:27 and 3John 4 are the other 2 telic-extents in which B is a figurative "end". John 15:13 and 1John 3:1 are telic-outcome and telic-extent. (I often use the predominant "outcome" to refer to any telic B).

A telescope illustrates what a telic *ina* shows. A telescope seems to bring a large remote object closer, so that a person can see it better. Likewise, a telic *ina* in A → B connects and relates a "remote" outcome B (result, end ...) to a "source" A. If a source-to-outcome relationship between A and B is clear, then the often non-telic "that or to" may also be clear translations; but IF God or John is informing the reader about a less obvious A–B relationship, then we NEED EXTRA WORDS to express it and not create misinformation. English words that show a telic *ina* are capitalized on p. 18 (SO THAT, IN ORDER THAT...).

The specific issue for translators has been translating *ina* B as if it identifies A like *oti* B (*oti* B identifies A in 234 of John's 413 uses of *oti*: 57%). In most contexts, the relationship of A and B is well understood and is not considered, but in about 22 spiritually informative *ina*-verses (SIV's), LEARNING the RELATIONSHIP of A with B is a key issue, and John could have used *oti* to show it (in 10 to 20, this A-B relationship is clearer or less vital). As Chapter 2 can show, rightly identifying Jesus' and our food and His work for us to do is practical: we CANNOT PRODUCE God's full OUTCOME while IGNORING His revelation of its SOURCE. Trying or striving to fix a real long-term problem but never fixing its source produces failure and superficiality. (Chapters 3 and 4 will show likewise).

What We Have Seen and Where We Go From Here

In Chapter 2 you saw the telic meaning of *ina*: to connect a source or start to a possible or projected outcome or extent. You also saw how a telic *ina* provides a profoundly different meaning to John 4:34 and 6:29 and very little change to 6 other *ina*-statements. In Chapters 1-2 you have seen significant connections between key verses in John 1, 3, 4, 5, and 6 with the theme in John 15: to abide or stay in Jesus and His love. All that Jesus DID on earth came out of His special fellowship with His Father, and all that we SHOULD DO should also come out of our special life and fellowship with Him in Jesus.

Chapter 3 shows the tight connection within John 13:33-15:17 with this same theme that we have been seeing in John's Gospel.

Chapter 3

Jesus' New Command in John 13-15

We have been finding John 15's theme connecting bigger pieces of John than we normally associate. Here we shall find that John 13:34 and John 15 are far more tightly connected than is normally assumed.

Jesus' New Commandment in John 13:34 and in 15:1-17

The small context of Jesus' new commandment in John 13:34 (v. 33-36) helps us to realize that a far larger context (13:33-15:17) is the best relevant context of v. 34. Here is John 13:33-36:

> [33]"Little children, I am with you a little while longer. You will seek Me; and as I said to the Jews, now I also say to you, 'Where I am going, you cannot come.' [34]A new commandment I give to you, **that [ina]** you love one another, even as I have loved you, **that [ina]** you also love one another. [35]By this all men will know that you are My disciples, if you have love for one another." [36]Simon Peter said to Him, "Lord, where are You going?" Jesus answered, "Where I go, you cannot follow Me now; but you will follow later." (John 13:33-36)

Notice: Jesus introduced two huge issues (2 bombs!) to His disciples in the underlined part of v. 33 and in v. 34 before the first *ina*: (1) they cannot come where He is going, and (2) He gives them a new commandment. In v. 36 Peter jumped on issue 1, and Jesus started explaining it in 13:36, which CONTINUED UNTIL the END of John 14.

{ What are the next commands? 3 imperative commands in 14:1 fit neatly in v. 2-3: Jesus said explicitly He will go to His Father and prepare a place for them with Him that they will go later when He comes for them (issue 1). Jesus' commands in 14:11 (for the disciples to believe in the relationship of Him with His Father or believe Their works) have a context of the disciples learning Jesus' relationship with His Father and God's full provision of His

Spirit for Jesus' disciples while He is not physically with them (v. 8-31). John 14's end (v. 27-31) gives them and us vital truths especially for their impending crisis when Jesus would be physically taken away from them. Then John 15:1-3 provides the picture of the Vine and the branches. His word cleansing the 11 (15:3) connects back to Jesus' declaring them clean in John 13:10. }

Then John 15:4-17, especially v. 4 and 9-10, gives a key command: "**Abide in Me, and I in you.**" Jesus commands us to abide in the life-giving, loving fellowship in Jesus, which was introduced in John 13:34 but was not stated until John 15:4. As we saw on p. 5-6, 15:9 also commands us disciples to abide in this fellowship by saying "**Abide in My love**"; and 15:10 explains what "abide in My love" means by its key feature (fully obey God), so that we can know if we truly are "abiding".

Moreover, the bold Greek in John 13:34 and 15:12 is identical despite differences in many translations:

[34a]A new commandment I give to you, **that [ina] you love one another, even as I have loved you**, [b]that [ina] you also love one another. (John 13:34)
[12a]This is My commandment, [b]that [ina] you love one another, just as I have loved you. (John 15:12)

With a consistently telic ina, John 15:4 is Jesus' first command after 13:33 that would fit His new commandment. The "This" that begins v. 12 refers to the whole life-giving abiding fellowship in v. 4-11, and specifically the commands in v. 4 and 9-10. V. 4 and 9-10 combine to form a single command in v. 4-11 that is the commandment (source A) for the bold underlined projected outcome (B) in both John 13:34a and 15:12b. Both verses call the fellowship described in 15:4-11 a single commandment (I often shorten it to the "abide in Me" [stay in Me] in John 15:4 and 1John 2:28). Moreover, both John 15:13-17 and John 13:34b (after its bold) show that loving as Jesus loved us disciples should cause our further loving one another, but 15:13-17 shows more about "as I have loved you" (15:12b, 13:34a) than 13:34b shows.

In this way we can see that <u>Jesus' new commandment</u> in John 13:34 <u>is</u> to <u>stay in this</u> whole life-giving <u>fellowship in John 15:1-17</u>, with v. 13-17 adding to the foundation in v. 1-12a and to its outcome in v. 12b. The "vine and branches" picture in John 15:1-6 strongly tells us, STAY CONNECTED to JESUS. And 15:17 concludes all of v. 1-17 with a statement that rarely makes it from the literal Greek into English: **"These things** I _command_ you, **so that** [**ina**] _you will love one another"_ (ESV, which handles well the bold English). Jesus again commands us to stay in this whole life-giving fellowship with Him and His Father described in v. 1-16, and v. 17 again emphasizes that this special fellowship should <u>produce this telic _ina_'s outcome</u>: loving one another.

Rightly identifying Jesus' new commandment is vital. For example, every translation of John 13:34 that I have seen commands us to love one another; and their translation of all John leaves us with "try harder to obey His command" if <u>long-term</u> we are not loving as we should. But a telic _ina_ in John 13:33-15:17 shows us God's solution: <u>first truly connect to and stay with God through Jesus</u>, and <u>then we shall love others better by His loving Spirit</u> (this solution includes keeping our hearts open to Him for His cleansing, purifying, and healing). Recall (p. 7, 13-15, 20): Father God was <u>the Source</u> of <u>all Jesus did</u>, and I can <u>love as Jesus loved</u> in my life with God that is like Jesus' life with Him.

I realize what this section can do to nearly every reader. _"A new commandment I give to you, **that** <u>you love one another</u>..."_ seems so simple and "obviously right". Consistently translating _ina_ in Jesus' new commandment verses probably has surprised me the most (I also read Bibles in English): now I realize "love one another..." is an OUTCOME of His new command. Instead of 13:34 disproving John's consistent use of _ina_, 13:34's context amazingly reveals the same command and theme we saw in Chapters 1-2: <u>stay</u> in Jesus and in His love.

John 15:1-17: Jesus' Commandment to Stay in Our Fellowship in Him

So far we have seen parts of John 1, 3, 4, 5, 6, and 13 meaningfully connect to John 15:1-17, and especially to 2 key commands in v. 4-10. Therefore we should examine 15:1-17 as a theme in John's Gospel.

V. 1-17 contain 8 *ina*'s the King James Version translates as "that", and the context of only 3 of these *ina*'s makes John's telic meaning of *ina* so clear that the NAS translates *ina* as "so that". "That" might be a shortened form of "so that", but often is a connective word that does not suggest a meaning like "so that". This causes a great loss of meaning in 5 *ina*-verses in v. 1-17 (v. 8, 12, 13, 16 [first *ina* twice], 17).

Therefore as I quote the NAS below, I insert an underlined "**so**" in front of the NAS' "that" to show a telic source-outcome relationship of John's consistent *ina* (the NAS translates these 5 *ina*'s as "that"). I also put words for each *ina* in **bold** and add comments within [brackets] about Greek antecedents, words, a commandment (an imperative), or the thrust of a verse. With these adjustments to the NAS translation, here is Jesus speaking the vital John 15:1-17:

¹*I am the true vine, and My Father is the vinedresser.*

²*Every branch in Me that does not bear fruit, He takes away; and every branch that bears fruit, He prunes it **so that** it may bear more fruit* [God's pruning produces this outcome: the branch bears more fruit].

³*You are already clean because of the word which I have spoken to you* [as stated on p. 22, v. 3 explains the cleansing in 13:10 and 13:1-17].

⁴*Abide in Me, and I in you* [the first command in John 15, and the first imperative in John 13-15 that fits as Jesus' new commandment]. *As the branch cannot bear fruit of itself unless it abides in the vine, so neither can you unless you abide in Me.*

⁵*I am the vine, you are the branches; he who abides in Me and I in him, he bears much fruit, for* [oti] *apart from Me you can do nothing.*

⁶*If anyone does not abide in Me, he is thrown away as a branch and dries up; and they gather them, and cast them into the fire and they are burned.*

⁷*If you abide in Me, and My words abide in you, ask* [the second

command in John 15, but some texts show an indicative] *whatever you wish, and it shall be done for you.*

⁸My Father is glorified [reliably answered prayer according to His will provides a tangible manifestation of His character and special presence] *by this* [in our abiding fellowship in Jesus in v. 4 and 7, we ask Father God so that He answers], <u>**so**</u> ***that*** *you bear much fruit, and so prove to be My disciples* [our asking and receiving glorifies God, and both set up or produce the outcome that we bear much fruit, which will prove that we are Jesus' disciples (13:35, p. 21)].

⁹Just as My Father has loved Me, I have also loved you; abide in My love [the third imperative in v. 1-17, and the second way to say Jesus' new commandment].

¹⁰If you keep My commandments [notice the plural, which I believe go far beyond v. 4, 7, and 9 to be <u>all that He tells us</u>], *you will abide in My love; just as I have kept My Father's commandments and abide in His love* [v. 10 shows a key to what it means to "<u>abide in My love</u>" (v. 9)].

¹¹These things I have spoken to you **so that** *My joy may be in you, and* <u>so</u> *that* [no word: repeating *ina* can add clarity in English] *your joy may be made full* [Jesus' words to them lead to their being full of His joy].

¹²This is My commandment [notice its singular: by examining the context back to John 13, I conclude that this commandment is "Abide in Jesus" in John 15:4, 9], <u>**so**</u> *that you love one another, just as I have loved you* [a key <u>outcome</u> of the commandment "abide in Jesus" is to <u>love one another as He loved them</u>: *ina*'s <u>source A</u> can include all of v. 1-12a].

¹³Greater love has no one than this [loving as Jesus loved us], <u>**so**</u> ***that*** *one lay down his life for his friends* [our loving as He has loved us (v. 12, 13a's "this") should ultimately lead each of us to lay down one's life for his friends, like Jesus did for His disciples – His friends <u>if v. 14</u>].

¹⁴You are My friends if you do what I command you.

¹⁵No longer do I call you slaves; for [oti] *the slave does not know what his master is doing; but I have called you friends, for* [oti] *all things that* [not *ina* or *oti*] *I have heard from My Father I have made known to you.*

¹⁶You did not choose Me but I chose you, and appointed you <u>**so that**</u> *you would go and bear fruit, and* <u>so</u> *that* [no *ina*, but repeats v. 16's first *ina*] *your fruit would remain* [the eventual outcome of Jesus' choosing and appointing us should be our bearing <u>abiding</u> (lasting) fruit], **so that** *whatever you ask of the Father in My name He may give to you* [bearing lasting fruit in our lives sets up the outcome of <u>further asking and receiving</u> from the Father in Jesus name, which leads to our loving one another better (as the summary below shows)].

[17]*This* [literally, "*these things*": I believe they include all the commands in the v. 1-16 fellowship that I summarize after this quote of v. 1-17] *I command you, **so that** you love one another* [Jesus' 3 commandments in v. 4, 7, and 9 with their follow-through in v. 1-16 lead to the outcome of our loving one another more effectively].

The poorly-seen start of the abiding fellowship in v. 1-17 is God's choosing and appointing us in v. 16: as Jesus explains in John 6:44-45 (I also explain on p. 10, 16-17), God's unseen work sets us up to do His explicit commands in this fellowship (15:4, 7, 9, 17), and the rest of 15:1-17 provides a well-ordered, instructive picture. Here are key John 15:1-17's "source → outcome" relationships and "these things" that our Lord Jesus commands us in v. 17:

We start with God's choosing and appointing us (v. 16), and the picture of the Vine and branches with Jesus' word cleaning us (v. 1-6)

→ Jesus commands us to abide (= stay) in Him and He in us (v. 4, 7), and this includes letting His words abide in us to clean us (v. 3, 7)

→ Jesus commands or tells us to ask our Father for whatever we wish, and we will receive from Him (v. 7)

→ our bearing much fruit (v. 8: "by this" refers to v. 7, coming after it and before the rest of v. 8 in the Greek)

→ our being further commanded to abide (stay) in Jesus' love (v. 9) – this abiding in His love features keeping His commandments (v. 10)

→ our loving one another as Jesus has loved us (v. 12)

→ our laying down our lives for our friends (v. 13's "this" and "greater love no one has" can refer to Jesus' love for us in v. 12 and also be a telic-extent: how far greater love might "figuratively go" [= extend])

→ our bearing fruit that remains or abides (v. 16: this comes from Jesus' choosing and appointing us earlier in v. 16, from our asking and receiving in v. 7-8, and from our loving like Jesus in v. 12-13)

→ our further asking and receiving in our abiding relationship with Jesus (v. 16's final *ina* – as we have continued to learn from Him)

→ our loving one another even more effectively than in v. 12 (as we grow in wisdom and power to love more like Jesus loved: v. 16-17, and p. 22-23 show how 15:13-17 is like the last part of John 13:34).

I see 3 explicit commandments (v. 4, 9, and in many Greek texts, v. 7), and they were discussed as a foundation for this book (p. 5-9). "This" (*tauta* = these things) in v. 17 is <u>plural</u> and normally translated as plural: the singular item at the end of v. 17 (that you love one another) does <u>not identify</u> v. 17's first Greek word. V. 17 is a fitting conclusion: in v. 17 <u>Jesus commands</u> these things in v. 1-16 in a different way to help His disciples <u>stay in this life and fellowship</u> emphasized there.

Here I organize the "John 15 *ina*-content" with earlier discussions:

* P. 5-9 show the key command in v. 4, 7-10: stay (= abide) in Jesus and stay in His love.

* P. 12-17 show Jesus' and our true food in John 4-6, and John 6's work for His followers to stay in John 15's fellowship in Jesus.

* P. 21-22 show Jesus' same new commandment in both John 13:34 and 15:12: stay in Him and in His love.

* P. 22-23 provide an overview of John 15:1-17 with the consistent *ina*.

* P. 24-26 discuss each verse in v. 1-17 using only telic *ina*'s.

A consistently telic *ina* in John 15:1-17 describes Jesus' new commandment in 13:34 and reveals the key missing theme in John's Gospel (it is also 1John's key theme). I believe that the key difference between the telic-*ina* picture and major translations of v. 1-17 is to <u>shift our foundation and source</u> from loving one another <u>to abiding in Jesus</u>. However, I also point out that a telic *ina* does <u>not reduce our calling</u> to <u>grow in our loving one another</u>. 15:10 shows clearly: to <u>abide or stay</u> in this loving fellowship with God in Jesus <u>includes keeping His commandments</u>, which include love one another. But a telic *ina* in v. 1-17 shows us <u>HOW</u> to move <u>long-term</u> <u>into loving</u> one another <u>more effectively</u>: by <u>staying or abiding in our</u> special loving <u>fellowship with Him</u>, the Source of our best love.

Notice that many Christian groups emphasize this theme: a life-giving fellowship with God through Jesus is <u>the source of our loving</u>

fellowship with one another. Other Scriptures are normally used as the basis for this theme, and too many miss it. Here we see that the Greek Scriptures for John 15:1-17 offer a strong basis for it: a true fellowship with God is the SOURCE of our best loving one another.

Jesus' True Food As a True "New Testament Mystery"

You are now in a good position to see Jesus' true food in John 4-6 and John 15's "stay in Jesus" as a real "New Testament mystery": fully unseen in John 1-4, naturally unrecognizable hints provided in John 5 (but easily seen with "hindsight"), a partial unveiling in John 6, more in John 10 (p. 51-52), and Jesus' open revelation in John 13-17 (really by John 15:17, but also 17:20-23). Jesus' open revelation shifts the focus from true food to staying in this life (fellowship) with our Father and Jesus that is like They had with each other. In it we eat our true food, so that we abide in Him (John 6:55-57), hear Him, see what He is doing and wants us to do, and thereby do it with Him in our lives on earth.

Conclusions from a Telic Ina in Key Scriptures in John's Gospel

So far we have seen a very different meaning that a consistently telic translation of 9 ina's in 8 verses provides for those Scriptures. But notice that these newly-found meanings fit into a Biblically-sound, Gospel-consistent theme: as a top long-term priority, we first connect to God (or re-connect if this fits) and stay connected with Him in the life and fellowship with Him and one another that He makes available to us in Jesus. God in us gives the power for us to stay in Him. The Source of our best love will work with us and in us to produce essential outcomes of our close fellowship: obey all that Jesus tells us, and love one another and believe in Jesus increasingly and more effectively. (In the first outcome, we keep His commands and live by the words from His mouth, so that we work with Him as we do all He sends us to do).

Chapter 4

Jesus' Telic Praying in John 17

Jesus' prayer in John 17 has the greatest concentration of John's *ina*'s: 9%, or 19 of his 213 *ina*'s. All are source-outcome telic (Chapter 8), but I believe only 6 *ina*'s in 5 verses need the special consideration in this chapter to complete our survey of key new insights revealed by a consistently telic *ina* in John's Gospel. We shall see the same simple remedy: a "source–outcome" connective like "so that" instead of an ambiguous "that" or "to", which is often not read like John used *ina*.

Realizing a Key Outcome That Should Be Produced in Our Eternal Life

John 17:3 clearly is a spiritually informative verse about eternal life:

This is eternal life, **that** *[ina] they may* **know** *You, the only true God, and Jesus Christ whom You have sent.* (John 17:3)

A telic *ina* in v. 3 shows that relationally coming to know God and Jesus (*ina*'s B) is a key outcome of eternal life (*ina*'s A). This helps us see a major work that should be starting in our eternal life on earth: verses like John 3:36 show eternal life as an ongoing present tense for those believing in Jesus. V. 3's Greek word for "know" (*ginōskō*) shows why it is good to realize "*ginōskō* God" is a potential outcome of eternal life. *Vine's Complete Expository Dictionary* contrasts its first two words for "know": *ginōskō* has special connotations that *oida* (a word for "know" that John also used often) does not have. *Oida* is to perceive fully or as a fact, but *ginōskō* increases especially by relationship of the knower with the one known, and *ginōskō* suggests the knower's increasing experiential knowledge and approval of the known.

Realizing that "eternal life is a key source with *ginōskō* God as its outcome" can help us confirm with Him that it has already started and is increasing: we should be using our eternal life to get to *ginōskō* Him better. In contrast, "that" in 17:3 (as if *ina* were *oti*) shows that *ginōskō* God is a key part of eternal life that comes with it. A telic *ina* in v. 3 gives emphasis and purpose to what should be developing in our own eternal life on earth: the telic source A → outcome B (p. 17-20).

John 17:3 brings out that getting to know God better relationally should be produced in our abiding fellowship with Him in John 15:1-17. We can see this as a connection of John 17 to John's unveiled theme.

Jesus' Prayer in John 17:11 for This Outcome: God's Unity in the 11

Jesus was directly speaking only to His 11 disciples in John 15, and we shall see that John 17:20-26 explicitly extends His words to us believers today. Jesus' prayer for His 11 disciples in John 17:11 with glimpses of its fulfillment in Acts gives a confirmed meaning of our unity that is like God's unity in John 14-15 and 17:21, 22, and 23:

> [11]*I am no longer in the world; and yet they themselves are in the world, and I come to You. Holy Father, KEEP them in Your name, the name which You have given Me,* **that** *[ina] THEY MAY BE ONE EVEN AS WE ARE.* (John 17:11)

Father God KEPT Jesus' 11 disciples in Their name, and this source led to its outcome: their special unity that is like God's oneness both in John 14-15 and like Jesus prayed for us in John 17:20-23.

Receive the Source to Move into the Impossible Outcomes in 17:20-23

John 17:21-23 contain the final 4 *ina*'s in John's Gospel where I see a huge loss of content caused by translating *ina* as "that" if the content does not display *ina*'s consistently telic "source → outcome" meaning:

> [20]*I do not ask on behalf of these alone, but for those also who believe in Me through their word;* [21]**that** *they may all be one; even as You, Father, are in Me and I in You,* [b]**that** *they also may be in Us,*

so that the <u>world may believe</u> that You sent Me. [22]The <u>glory</u> which <u>You have given Me</u> <u>I have given to them</u>, [b]***that*** they may be <u>one</u>, just <u>as We are one</u>. [23a]*I in them and You in Me*, [b]***that*** they may be <u>perfected in unity</u>, **so that** the <u>world may know</u> that You sent Me, and loved them, even as You have loved Me. (John 17:20-23. All 6 bold conjunctions are *ina*, and the 2 "so that" are <u>easy-to-see</u> telic.)

Jesus prayed John 17:11 for and revealed John 15:1-17 to only His 11 disciples. V. 20 <u>extends both to</u> <u>all of us who believe in Jesus</u>. His praying in v. 20 is a source for v. 21's first *ina*'s outcome: <u>we</u> are <u>all one like</u> He and His Father are one (John 10:38; <u>14:</u>10-11, <u>20</u>; <u>15:4</u>). This is a <u>real</u> outcome – like He <u>prayed</u> <u>and</u> <u>fulfilled</u> <u>for the 11</u> in 17:11 (p. 30).

17:20-21a is the second *ina*'s source. "Our <u>being one</u> with <u>Father God in us</u> <u>like</u> <u>He was in Jesus</u>" (second *ina*'s source) should lead to its outcome: we are "in Them". V. 21 and 23 add Father God to Jesus in His *"<u>abide</u> in Me, and <u>I</u> in you"* command in John 15:4: 17:20-21 shows more about <u>getting us in Them</u> and v. 22-23 on <u>Them fully in us</u>. John 15:4-10 adds an emphasis of <u>our need to stay</u> in this life. Staying in our life in Jesus and His Father is a source for v. 21's third *ina*'s outcome: the world gets a good opportunity to believe that our Father sent Jesus (the NAS, ESV, RSV, and some others translate this *ina* well).

In v. 22, Father God is the <u>source</u> of <u>Jesus' glory</u> that <u>He gave us</u> in order to (***ina***) make us one like They are one (v. 21, 22-23). Consider: <u>Biblical glory</u> is the <u>manifestation of inner qualities</u> <u>caused by</u> <u>God's special presence</u>. What is the <u>chief glory on earth</u> Father God gave Jesus? To have God's presence and full nature within Jesus' human body, and to manifest God's true nature to the people around Jesus and interacting with Him (which He did by eating His true food: p. 12-14). John 15:4-10, 17:23, and other Scriptures show that God is within us believers in Jesus, but Scriptures like Eph. 4:11-16 show that we corporately have <u>not yet</u> <u>manifested Him well</u>. (V. 11-16 reveal that our true corporate <u>standard</u> is the fully Christ-like Body of Christ: Jesus manifested God's true nature to those interacting with Him).

A telic *ina* in v. 22 shows Jesus' intent for His glory given us to lead to our oneness that is like Theirs: *[b]ina they may be one, just as We are one. [23a]I in them and You in Me…".* His glory He has given us is this *ina*'s source: manifesting Their true nature can be the key (as a source) to producing our oneness that is like Jesus had with His Father.

V. 22's telic *ina* helps us FIX the SOURCE of the problem so that we get v. 22's long-term solution. If we manifest Him well – we have not so far – then v. 21-23 will proceed. Our key work is to seek God with His special loving presence to be manifested in our lives (John 5:19, 5:30, 14:10-11, 15:4-10, p. 7): manifesting His true nature is a key part of our work with Him in us to produce v. 22-*ina*'s outcome – we become one!

Consider v. 23's first *ina*: *"[22b]they may be one, just as We are one. [23]I in them and You in Me, **that** they may be perfected in unity…* God's continued presence and work in us and coming out of us provide the source for the first *ina* outcome in both 17:21 and 17:23: we can get perfected in unity as we let Him keep working in us, as in John 15:4-17 and 13:34. God IN US empowers us to stay in Him. Our unity in 17:23's outcome is the source for v. 23's last *ina* outcome: the world would know that Father God sent Jesus and loved us like Him (the NAS and a few others translate this *ina* well, as some do v. 21's "*ina* the world…").

All of this shows how 17:20-23 extends John's unveiled theme (stay in Jesus) into John 17. (17:21ab, 22, and 23a are the 4 key telic *ina*'s).

The NAS and NIV also well translate John 17:26's *ina*, but we can get great insight for our discussion of John 17 here: *"and **I have made Your name known** to them, and **will make it known**, **so that** the love with which You loved Me may be in them, and I in them."* The key is in the meaning of "Your name": Jesus' Father's nature and character that Jesus has made known to the 11 and to us. This helps us understand the *"keep them in Your name, the name which You have given Me"* in John 17:11 (p. 30): put character or nature in both verses to get very meaningful statements. In contrast, a name as a label to address someone provides head-knowledge that is spiritually useless.

The John 15 Theme Extending into John 18-21

Jesus' great love for His people shown in John 18-21 explicitly demonstrates the "greater love no one has" in John 15:12-13:

> [12]*This is My commandment, **so that** you love one another, just as I have loved you.* [13]*Greater love has no one than this, **so that** one lay down his life for his friends.* (John 15:12-13; and as on p. 25, I add the bold underlined "so" to each NAS translation of *ina* in v. 12-13.)

More specifically, John 18-19 shows how much Jesus was willing to suffer in order to lay down His life for us, so that He could justly provide good for us. John 20-21 shows glimpses of His love for His people after His resurrection: they show His love continuing like John 1-19 shows.

Conclusions from Examining a Few Ina-Verses in John's Gospel

A telic *ina* (= source → outcome) in Chapters 1-4 helps us see:

* that Jesus' food was His life-giving fellowship in which He saw and heard what His Father was doing – this fellowship was the source of an outcome, which was everything Jesus did (John 5:19, 5:30, 14:10);

* that our food in Jesus is like Jesus' food in His Father in John 6:26-58 and 15:1-17 (especially 6:57 and 15:9-10): we eat His words to us as we abide (= stay) in the life and fellowship in Jesus that He gives us;

* that the work of God (John 6:27) is for His true food: we do what we need to stay in our fellowship with God in Jesus (keep receiving Him), and it leads to 6:29's vital outcome that we increasingly believe in Him;

* that Jesus commands us to abide in Him and to abide in His love – we will abide in His love if we keep His commandments as He kept His Father's commandments and abided in His love (John 15:4, 9-10);

* that Jesus' new commandment is to abide in Him (stay in the life and fellowship shown in John 15:1-17) – this causes our love for one another to grow so much that all can see it (John 17:20-23 on p. 30-32, John 13:35 on p. 21);

* that this life and fellowship with Father God, Jesus His Son, and other believers who love one another in John 15:1-17 is a theme in John's Gospel, starting with John 1:12 and 3:7 (truly receiving Jesus and being born again, p. 9-10) and extending into John 17-21 (Chapter 4);

* that <u>love one another</u> is <u>an outcome of our fellowship</u> with our Father and our Lord Jesus, so that we <u>FIX a long-term lack</u> by connecting to and staying with the <u>best Source of love for one another</u> in order to love well;

* that asking-and-receiving in this fellowship – in which we stay in Him and let Him and His words stay in us (15:7) – is a major way to glorify our Father and produce much fruit (15:8);

* that staying fully in this fellowship leads to further (better) asking-and-receiving and loving one another and producing lasting fruit (15:16);

* that a key purpose and <u>outcome of eternal life</u> – to get to know God better and better – is to <u>start</u> in our <u>lives on earth</u> as we <u>abide in our life and fellowship with God and one another</u> in John 15 and 17:3;

* that Jesus' giving us His glory is a key to producing the outcome of a special unity that is like Jesus with His Father – a telic *ina* helps us FIX the SOURCE (manifest His nature) of the problem (lacking unity) in order for us to get its true long-term solution for us and the world.

In Chapters 1-4 we see that a telic *ina* reveals John 15's "abide in Jesus" or "stay in My love" command and picture as a vital theme of John's Gospel. We also see its 15 *ina*'s that provide the predominant difference of a consistent (purely telic) *ina* from the usual translations of each *ina*: in contrast to the translations, EVERY *ina* can easily reveal a "source A → outcome B" relationship (telic, p. 17-20). From Chapter 8 I add: in <u>all</u> of John's 213 *ina*'s in his Gospel, 3 Epistles, and Revelation, I can see a good "source-A *ina* outcome-or-extent-B" meaning for <u>every *ina*</u> that John used.

Chapters 5-6 show the 10 *ina*'s in John's Epistles and Revelation where I see the greatest changes by a telic *ina*. We shall also see John 15's theme in 1John: this <u>abiding life or fellowship with</u> Father God, Jesus, and believers who love one another is Jesus' New Commandment, a key theme in John's Gospel, and also the key theme of 1John (Chapter 5). 1-2John provide much evidence that initial 1John receivers <u>were WELL GROUNDED in this theme</u> and needed <u>only</u> encouragements and <u>reminders</u> to <u>stay in Jesus</u>.

Chapter 5

The John 15 Fellowship in All 1John

1John 1:1-3 describes a life-giving fellowship with Father God, His Son Jesus Christ, and other believers who are loving one another. Details in 1John help us see that this is <u>the fellowship in John 15:1-17</u>. In 1John 1:3-4, John shows that <u>he is writing them an invitation</u> to <u>join or rejoin or stay in</u> this special fellowship. Consider v. 1-4:

*¹What was from the beginning, what we have heard, what we have seen with our eyes, what we have looked at and touched with our hands, concerning the <u>Word of Life</u> – ²and the <u>life was manifested</u>, and we have seen and testify and proclaim to you the <u>eternal life</u>, which <u>was with the Father</u> and was <u>manifested to us</u> – ³what we have seen and heard we proclaim to you also, **so that** [**ina**] <u>you too may have fellowship</u> with us; and indeed <u>our fellowship is with the Father, and with His Son Jesus Christ</u>. ⁴These things we write, **so that** [**ina**] our joy may be made complete. (1John 1:1-4)*

Identifying 1John's Singular Commandment: John 15:1-17

In 1John 2:7-8, John says that he is writing them a <u>commandment</u> (singular!) with certain features – an <u>emphasized word</u> they had <u>heard</u>:

*⁷Beloved, I am <u>not writing a new commandment</u> to you, but <u>an **old** commandment</u> which <u>you have **had from the beginning**</u>; the <u>old **commandment**</u> is the **word** which **you have heard**. ⁸On the other hand, I am <u>writing a **new** commandment</u> to you, which is <u>true in Him and in you</u>, because the darkness is passing away and the true Light is already shining. (1John 2:7-8)*

John wrote a commandment both old and new to his "receivers": all he invited in 1:3-4 to <u>join or rejoin</u> the intimate life-giving fellowship <u>with God and those already in</u> this fellowship with Him and John. They <u>had</u>

had and had heard this commandment from the beginning (when each receiver began life in Jesus). And this truly was a new command because they had grown to be different from when they had begun their life in Jesus. Therefore darkness had already begun to pass away and the true Light had already started to shine in their life with Jesus.

Jesus gives us many commands. What is this single command that John refers to 3 times and that his initial receivers (the initial 1John readers or hearers) had heard and did understand this reference to it?

Most translators effectively assume John used *ina* B to identify A: non-telic, p. 17-20. They assume 1John 3:23 and 4:21 are commands to love one another instead of an outcome of the true commandment that John referred to in 2:7-8. But in Chapters 2-4 we find that *ina* B is never needed to identify A in verses most affected in John's Gospel; and in Chapters 5-6 we find that *ina*'s assumed meaning veils the same vital theme in 1John that this meaning veils in John's Gospel.

This theme in John's Gospel very well fits every verse in 1John. In this section I show how I conclude that "Jesus' New Commandment" to abide in Him (John 15) is a far better single commandment. We shall see how well this command to receivers fulfills the features of 1John 2:7-8 and all singular-command verses in 1John, and fits into John's purposes for writing 1John (1:3-4; 2:1, 12-13, 21, 26; 5:13 – all quoted on p. 41-42). On p. 40-42, I explain my conclusions for 1John's "from the beginning", initial 1John receivers, and John's purposes for 1John.

As we are commanded in John 15 to abide in Jesus (15:4) and to abide in His love (15:9-10), so we are also commanded in 1John 2:28:

> [28]*Now, little children,* **ABIDE IN HIM**, *so that* [**ina**] *when He appears, we may have confidence and not shrink away from Him in shame at His coming.* (1John 2:28)

2:28 is only 1John's second imperative (a commandment). Let us see how well it fits as "His commandment" (singular!) that 1John refers to three times (1John 2:7-8, 3:23, 4:21). Consider 2:7-8 (p. 35).

"Abide in Jesus" – stay in the life-giving fellowship with Him that we saw described in John 15:1-17 – is a very likely commandment and teaching these believers HEARD at the beginning of their life with God through Jesus. Notice how useful it is for new believers today to realize what "abide in Jesus" means! Stay (abide or remain) in Jesus gets a new meaning in each new temptation to not obey His word (2:8, 3:24).

Therefore this single old-new command to abide in Him fits 1John 2:7-8 very well. Now consider "HIS COMMANDMENT" in 1John 3:23:

[22]and whatever we ask we receive from Him, because [oti] we keep His commandments and do the things that are pleasing in His sight. [23]This is **His commandment**, **that** [ina] we believe in the name of His Son Jesus Christ, and love one another, just as He commanded us. [24]The one who **keeps His commandments ABIDES IN HIM, and He in him**. We know by this that [oti] He abides in us, by the Spirit whom He has given us. (1John 3:22-24)

Translating ina as "that" in 3:23 has been the usual option, but has major problems (p. 38). Ina as "so that" fits amazingly well. 1John 2:28 freshly commands 1John receivers: abide in Him. 2:28 is far away from 3:23, but 3:24 shows that 2:28's command is well connected. 3:24 merely REMINDS: "keep His commandments" (v. 22, 24) is a key part of abiding in God. Its insertion into v. 24 after v. 23 with no explanation shows that John expected his receivers to know well that abiding in God is "His commandment" and shows how "This" in v. 23 refers to v. 22. 3:22-24 gives further evidence of referring to the same truth as John 15:7-12: both 15:7-10 and 3:22-24 contain ask-and-receive promises contingent on this abiding in God or Jesus, in which we keep His commandments and seek to do His will (p. 5-9; v. 22, 24 above).

Now consider the likely foundation in Christ of the initial receivers of 1John: as shown explicitly on p. 40-42, they most likely heard many commandments that included (1) believe in the name of the Father's Son Jesus Christ and (2) love one another and (3) abide in Him – stay in the fellowship shown in John 15, 1John 1:1-4, and all 1John. 3:24 reminds receivers: keeping His commands is a part of abiding in Jesus, and so the previous commands 1-2 (*"just as He commanded us"*, aorist indicative, earlier than 3:23) fit into command 3. This abiding fellowship in Jesus is so vital for 1John that it is written 4 times in 4:12-16 (below) – in a context of 1John's final singular commandment in 4:21.

For the above reasons, I conclude: John knew that God gave initial 1John receivers many commands, and that "His commandment" in 3:23 included keeping all of them (John 15:9-10, 1John 3:22, 24). We are starting to see the evidence in 1John that these receivers needed ONLY REMINDERS of the fellowship described in John 15.

Assuming *ina* B identifies "His commandment" in v. 23 – translating *ina* as "that" – has major problems. It assumes that John miscounted (very careless) or added a second commandment as an afterthought, but 1John is so deep and exact. Translating *ina* as if it were *oti* in v. 23 (that or to) has another problem: "believe" is not a commanding imperative, but a contingent subjunctive (should, would, might, may …). A Greek subjunctive after *ina* in v. 23 provides exactly the opposite emphasis fitting for a command (p. 56-57 further explain this).

Therefore a non-telic *ina* ("that") in 3:23 has major problems, but is the usually chosen option. Why? Not seeing a command a little before v. 23, translators translate *ina* as an ambiguous "that". Then English readers SEE the same lack of command plus a "non-telic that", and conclude the same more easily. This issue needs to be re-examined!

Now let us see 1John's final "singular commandment" in 4:21 is set up by many abide statements:

*…if we love one another, **God abides in us**, and His love is perfected in us.* (1John 4:12b)

By this we know that [oti] **we abide in Him** *and* **He in us***, because [oti] He has given us of His Spirit.* (1John 4:13)

Whoever confesses that [oti] Jesus is the Son of God, **God abides in him***, and* **he in God***.* (1John 4:15)

We have come to know and have believed the love which God has for us. God is love, and the one who abides in love **abides in God***, and* **God abides in him***.* (1John 4:16)

[20]*...one who does* **not love his brother***...*<u>**cannot love God**</u>*...*[21]***And this commandment** *we have from Him,* **that** *[ina] the* <u>one who loves God</u> **should love his brother** *also.* [1]*Whoever believes that [oti] Jesus is the Christ is born of God, and* <u>**whoever loves the Father** *loves the child born of Him*</u>. (1John 4:20-5:1)

What is <u>this commandment</u>? A non-telic "that" for *ina* helps English readers <u>assume</u> that this commandment is v. 21's B after *ina*: *"the one who loves God should love his brother also."* But v. 21's "should love" is the subjunctive or indicative *agapa*, not the commanding imperative *agapatō*: 4:13-21 has <u>no command</u>. <u>A command in v. 21</u> also <u>fails to fit its context</u>: loving God but not his brother <u>cannot exist</u> (4:20); and in 5:1, *"<u>Whoever loves the Father</u> <u>loves the child born of Him</u>"*. <u>If I truly love God</u>, <u>then I love</u> my brother, God's child. 1Tim. 1:9 confirms that a command fails to fit here: a law is made for those who <u>may</u> disobey it.

In contrast to identifying this command (like *oti* would do), a telic *ina* in v. 21 shows that "the one loving God also loves his brother" is <u>an outcome of</u> "<u>this commandment</u>". Again, what is "this commandment" in 4:21? The 4 abiding statements in 4:12-16 combine with the other 2 singular commands in 1John to suggest "abide in God" – stay in Him!

Consider how "<u>this</u>" commandment fits v. 21: to "abide in God" is to stay in that loving, life-giving fellowship in 1John and John 15:1-17. In 1John and John 15, this "New Commandment" to <u>stay in Him</u> produces this outcome: <u>loving God and also his brother</u>. "Abide in God" fits 4:21 very well, as it also fits <u>every singular commandment</u> in 1John.

We have also <u>begun to see</u> that this <u>abiding in God</u> is <u>a theme of</u> 1John, and that <u>1John gives no need to assume *ina* B identifies its A</u>.

"The Beginning" in 1John, and 1John's Anticipated Receivers

In this section I explain my conclusions from verses in 1John about 2 issues that can help us appreciate the clear picture in 1John: first, his 3 meanings of "the beginning"; then John's anticipated (likely initial) 1John receivers (readers or hearers) and his purposes for them.

In 1John 1:1 and 2:13-14, "the beginning" refers to God. Therefore it refers to the beginning of His creation (in it God created time).

1John 3:8 says that *"...the devil has sinned from the beginning..."*, and I see two good meanings for 3:8: the devil's beginning in sin (I and many others believe this to be described in Ez. 28:15-17), or the devil's introducing sin into mankind through Adam and Eve (either fits well).

The third and most vital meaning of "the beginning" in 1John is the beginning of each believer's life in Jesus (1John 2:7, 2:24, 3:11):

*[7]Beloved, **I am** not **writing** a new commandment to you, but **an old commandment** which **YOU have HAD** from the beginning; the old commandment is **the word** which **YOU HAVE HEARD**.* (1John 2:7)

*[24]As for you, **let that abide in you** which **YOU HEARD** from the beginning. If what **YOU HEARD** from the beginning abides in you, you also will **ABIDE in the Son and in the Father**.* (1John 2:24)

*[11]For **this is the message** which **YOU HAVE HEARD** from the beginning, that [ina] we **should love one another**.* (1John 3:11)

This beginning is different for each of us: John's beginning when he first HEARD and had the commandment, word, or message came in John 15: before each initial receiver's beginning. All of their beginnings came before your or my beginning. My beginning was near to when I first received Jesus into my heart and life. A command or word that fits being HEARD from each believer's beginning – not before then – is to abide in Jesus, to STAY in the special fellowship in John 15 and 1John.

1John 2:12-14 shows John previously wrote 1John's anticipated receivers. Realizing that John knew what 1John's initial receivers had received at the beginning and foundation of their life in Christ Jesus can help us be sensitive to many statements he wrote them. As I read 1John 1:3-4, 2:1, 7-8, 12-14, 21, 24, 26-28, and 5:13 (all quoted below), I see initial 1John receivers as (1) having heard and received foundational teachings of Jesus that included many commands and "His commandment" to abide or stay in Him (they knew what it is!), and (2) also NEEDING REMINDERS and encouragement to stay in Him:

> [3]*what we have seen and heard we proclaim to you also, **so that [ina] you too** may **have fellowship with us**; and indeed **our fellowship is with the Father**, and **with His Son Jesus Christ**. [4]These things **we write**, **so that** [ina] our joy may be made complete.* (1John 1:3-4, p. 35)

> [1]*My little children, **I am writing these things** to you **so that** [ina] you may not sin.* (1John 2:1. P. 43-44 show its context, 1:9-2:6.)

> [7]*Beloved, **I am** not **writing** a new commandment to you, but an **old commandment** which **you have had from the beginning**; the old commandment is the **word** which **you have heard**. [8]On the other hand, **I am writing** a **new commandment** to you, which is true in Him and in you, because [oti] the darkness is passing away and the true Light is already shining.* (1John 2:7-8, also quoted on p. 35 and p. 40 [v. 7] and discussed on p. 35-37.)

> [12]***I am writing*** *to you, little children, because [oti] your sins have been forgiven you for His name's sake. [13]**I am writing** to you, fathers, because you know Him who has been from the beginning. **I am writing** to you, young men, because you have overcome the evil one. **I have written** to you, children, because you know the Father. [14]**I have written** to you, fathers, because you know Him who has been from the beginning. **I have written** to you, young men, because you are strong, and the word of God abides in you, and you have overcome the evil one.* (1John 2:12-14. Realize: all 3 "I am writing" in v. 12-13 are the Greek present tense (ongoing); all 3 "I have written" in v. 13-14 are the Greek indicative aorist tense [showing a completed past action: I wrote]; all 6 "because" are oti.)

> [19]*They **went out from us**, but they were **not really of us**; for if they had been of us, they would have remained with us; but they went out, **so that** [ina] it would be shown that [oti] they all are not of us. [20]But you have an anointing from the Holy One, and **you all know**. [21]I have not **written to you because you** do not know **the truth**, but because you do **know it**, and because no lie is of the truth.... [24]As for you, let that abide in you which **YOU HEARD** from the*

beginning. ***If*** *what* ***you heard from the beginning abides in you,*** *you also will* ***abide in the Son and in the Father****.* (1John 2:19-21, 24. All 3 "because" in v. 21 are *oti*.)

[26]***These things I HAVE WRITTEN TO YOU*** *concerning* ***those*** *who are* ***TRYING TO DECEIVE YOU****.* [27]*As for you, the* ***anointing*** *which* ***you received from Him abides in you,*** *and* ***you*** *have* ***no need for anyone to*** *[****ina****]* ***teach you****; but as* ***His anointing teaches you*** *about all things, and is true and is not a lie, and just* ***as it has taught you****,* ***you abide in Him****.* [28]*Now, little children,* ***ABIDE IN HIM****,* ***so that*** *[****ina****] when He appears, we may have confidence and not shrink away from Him in shame at His coming.* (1John 2:26-28. V. 26 is a key part of the context for 1John and a previous epistle.)

[13]*These things I* ***have written to you who believe*** *in the name of the Son of God,* ***so that*** *[****ina****] you may know that [****oti****] you have eternal life.* (1John 5:13)

I conclude that:

* John knew the basic beginning and foundation of his initial 1John receivers (readers or hearers) and had added to it (2:12-14, above);

* these readers had heard and received into their hearts the true God and His words (but some could be only starting this fellowship in 1:3-4, who could get John's "brief reminders" clarified by those already in it);

* what they had heard and received from their beginning in Him included many commandments and "His commandment" to abide (stay) in Him – His commandment included keeping all of His commandments and specifically love one another (1John 3:22-24 and John 15:4, 9-10);

* that liars had gone forth from John's group of real believers but not of them (2:19-29), and these deceivers had shaken and confused some of 1John's receivers enough to need to be invited back into their life-giving fellowship (2:26, 1:3-4); and

* John was writing them reminders and encouragement to stay in Jesus as they were commanded in the beginning of each one's life in Him.

In this Chapter 5 we have sometimes seen "love one another" and "believe in Jesus' name" as vital commandments, but they are not 1John's singular "His commandment" (3:23: Jesus commanded it in John 15), "this commandment" (4:21, after 4 reminders to abide in God in 4:12-16), or the "old-new commandment" (2:7-8 on p. 35-37).

Chapter 6

Spiritually Informative Verses in 1-2John

Clearly many verses in 1John quoted in Chapter 5 are "spiritually informative", and we can see that English-speaking believers today are not well informed about some of this vital content. In Chapter 6 we consider other key spiritually informative verses in 1-2John from our fresh perspective: the consistently telic *ina*, and Jesus' command in all 1John that its receivers are to "abide in Him" – stay in the life-giving fellowship in Him that includes keeping His commands and His provision to restore one if he fails (1:9-2:2 below). This commandment extends to us believers today. Scriptures in this section will supplement (not repeat) the 1John Scriptures in Chapter 5: 1:1-4; 2:7-8, 2:12-14, 2:19-21, 2:24, 2:26-28; 3:22-24; 4:12-16; 4:20-5:1, and 5:13.

1:5: *And this is the message we have heard from Him and announce to you,* **that** *[oti] God is light, and in Him there is no darkness at all.* "God is light and has no darkness in Him" specifically identifies both "this" and "the message we have heard from Him and announce to you". John used *oti* B to identify an unidentified "this" and the whole antecedent A – what *oti* normally does, but also what *ina* is usually assumed to do in John's spiritually informative *ina*-verses.

1:9-2:6: [9]*If we confess our sins, He is faithful and righteous* **to** *[ina] forgive us our sins and* **to** *[the previous ina translated again] cleanse us from all unrighteousness.* [10]*If we say that [oti] we have not sinned, we make Him a liar and His word is not in us.* [1]*My little children,* **I am writing these things** *to you* **so that** *[ina] you may not sin. And if anyone sins, we have an Advocate with the Father, Jesus Christ the righteous;* [2]*and He Himself is the propitiation for our sins; and not for ours only, but also for those of the whole world.* [3]*By this we know that [oti] we have come to know Him, if we keep His commandments.* [4]*The one who says, "[oti] I have come to know Him," and does not keep His commandments, is a* **liar***, and the truth is not in him;* [5]*but whoever* *keeps His word, in him the love of God has truly been perfected. By this we know that [oti] we are in Him:* *⁶the one who says he **abides in Him** ought himself to **walk in the same manner as He** [Jesus] **walked**.*

1:9-2:6 comments: This Scripture applies *ina*'s source → outcome in v. 9 (we confess sins and God's nature → He forgives and cleanses us) to initial 1John receivers and us who may have sinned (2:1-2). *Ina* B's desired outcome is we do not sin, but v. 1-2 remind us of His sacrifice to restore us if we did sin. 1:9-2:2 connects well with 2:3-6: it shows us how to recognize one who truly knows God from a liar. 1:5-2:6 focuses on oneself and self-deception (lying to oneself), and 2:4-4:6 focuses on recognizing other liars who come in the name of the truth.

2:3-2:6 is the transition between these two large sections of 1John. 2:6 provides perhaps the most vital information in this transition: *"the one who says he **abides in Him** ought himself to **walk in the same manner as He walked**."* John 5:19, 30 and 14:10 (p. 7) describe how He walked. 2:6 identifies the key feature of one truly abiding in Jesus in contrast to a lying deceiver, and v. 3-6 refer to the same truth Jesus declared in John 15:9-10 for "His New Commandment": *"⁹JUST **AS My Father has loved Me**, I have also loved you; **abide in My love**. ¹⁰If you **keep My commandments**, **you will abide in My love**; JUST AS I have **kept My Father's commandments and abide in His love**."*

2:19-29: 1John 2:19-21, 24 and 26-28 are quoted on p. 41-42, and these verses show enough of v. 19-29 to simply state my conclusion about this spiritually informative Scripture. We should realize that if people lack the foundation of a 1John receiver (discussed on p. 40-42), then they might need enough teaching about God and the truth in order to recognize and receive God, the truth, the anointing, and His Spirit, so that they can stay (abide) in Him. We can see again: realizing that John knew the foundation of his initial 1John receivers can help us receive right and not wrong spiritual information in the Scripture.

3:1: *See how great a love the Father has bestowed on us, ᵇthat [ina] we would be called children of God; and such we are. For this reason the world does not know us, because [oti] it did not know Him.* The Father's great love bestowed on us (A) leads to this outcome: we are called His children (*ina*'s source → outcome). What is a special way to see God's great love? Two verses earlier, 1John 2:28 commands us to stay or abide in Christ – a short way to identify the fellowship in 1:1-4 and in all of 1John. This abiding fellowship in Christ helps us see and experience the great love God gives us (2:28-3:1a = *ina*'s big source A). This great love to us extends so far (showing how great it is) that we could be called children of God (*ina*'s B), and John affirms we are.

3:5-8: *⁵You know that [oti]* **He appeared** *in order to [ina]* take away sins; *and in Him there is no* sin. *⁶No one who* **abides in Him** sins; *no one who* sins *has seen Him or knows Him.* *⁷Little children, make sure* no one deceives you; *the one who* practices righteousness *is righteous, just as He is righteous;* *⁸the one who* practices sin *is of the devil; for [oti] the devil has* sinned from the beginning. *⁶The* **Son of God** **appeared** *for* **this purpose,** *to [ina]* **destroy the works of the devil.**

The best choice I see for A of v. 8's *ina* is "our sin and its removal" in v. 5-8a: Jesus appeared to take away sins (v. 5); no one who abides in Him sins (v. 6: keeps sinning, Greek present tense); and the one practicing sin is of the devil, who sinned from the beginning (v. 8a).

1John 3:5-8a is a large source A and is "this purpose". Jesus appeared in order to produce these OUTCOMES: TAKE AWAY SINS (v. 5), and DESTROY the WORKS of the devil (v. 8). Both outcomes include the sins of people who sin. V. 6-7 show that CONTINUED sin disrupts our abiding in Jesus, and this agrees with John 15:5-6: to choose to disconnect from Him for a sin dries up abiding fellowship with Him. If God speaks to a believer (about a sin), refusing God or His voice disrupts his/her abiding life in Christ. V. 5-8 with a consistent (telic) *ina* in v. 8 show that JESUS' taking away sins and OUR turning from sins (not staying in them) are keys to destroying the works of the devil (the devil's real goal and work is to separate people from God for further damage, and tempting people to sin is a key way).

3:11: *For [oti]* this is the message *which* you have heard from the beginning, *that [ina]* we should love one another. As we saw (p. 40), "the beginning" in v. 11 is near when a believer began his life-giving fellowship with Jesus: before then, any believer was not hearing a message from God (*ina*'s source) that led to the outcome of loving one another (especially not at the other two "beginnings" in 1John).

What is v. 11's "message heard from the beginning" (near when any 1John receiver began his real life in Christ)? To stay or abide in Jesus is a short way to say, "stay in the whole life-giving fellowship in Him" that 1John describes and 1John 2:28 reminds (Chapter 5). I see 1John 3:11 concisely REMINDING believers to ABIDE in this fellowship with God and His true children, and this source A (this heard message) should lead into John 15's outcome B: we love one another.

4:7: *Beloved,* let us love one another… 1:5, 1:9-2:6, 2:19-29, 4:7, 4:12-17, 4:19, and 5:21 are not "*ina*-verses to explain", but inform us in ways to belong on this list. In Greek, the first person plural subjunctive by an authority can have the force of a command. I also see 4:7 as a commandment to love one another, but not as 1John's commandment.

In 1John 4:12-17 that follows, I quoted (p. 38-39) v. 12b, 13, 15, and

16 (3 "abide in God and God abide in us" statements in 4 verses) as the relevant context and antecedent for "this commandment" in v. 21. Here I shall quote only v. 16b of v. 13-16 in order to show better the tight connection between v. 12b and 16-17 with a gist of their context.

4:12b-17: *[12]...[b]if we love one another, God abides in us, and **His** love is perfected in us ...[16]...[b]the one who abides in love abides in God, and God abides in him. [17]By this, love is **perfected** with us, so that [ina] we may have confidence in the day of judgment; because [oti] as He is, so also are we in this world.* In v. 17a "this" refers to our abiding fellowship in v. 16b, v. 12-16, and all of 1John: in it love is perfected with us.

V. 12b-17's details add to John 13:34b: *"[34]A new commandment I give to you, that [ina] you love one another, even as I have loved you, [b]that [ina] you also love one another."* 4:12b-17 adds insight to 13:34's first to second outcome like John 15:12-17 (p. 22-27): our fellowship in God and He in us produces its outcome of loving one another, and loving one another in this fellowship causes it to increase further and better.

Consider this further. Jesus' command in John 13:34 (abide in Him) has a first OUTCOME: love one another. With this love, 1John 4:12b shows that God (1) abides in us and thereby (2) perfects His love in us. # 2 is 13:34's second OUTCOME: to love one another better. V. 16b starts like v. 12b (v. 12's love one another = v. 16's abide in love and in God) with the same double result: God abides in us and His love is perfected with us (v. 12b, 16b-17a). In "love is perfected with us" (v. 17a), "with" is "*meth*" and means "in our midst or among us" – another way to describe our growing in effective "loving one another".

Ina B in v. 17 shows love perfected with us producing an outcome: we would have confidence in the day of judgment. (*Oti* B is placed to show another source of our confidence: whom God has made us to be in this world. We shall see this remarkable *ina-oti* fit on p. 67.)

4:19: *We love, **because** [oti] He first loved us.* V. 19 clearly identifies the Source of our *agape* love: receiving His love. 4:7-5:3 emphasizes love like 1:5-4:6 emphasizes truth and 5:4-21 with 1:1-4 our life in God.

5:2b-3: *[2]...when we love God and observe His commandments. [3]For **this** is the love of God, **that** [ina] we keep His commandments; and His commandments are not burdensome.* The love of God (*ina*'s A) is the source of this OUTCOME: we keep His commandments (B). This truth is shown in 1John 4:19 (5 verses back), *"We love, because He first loved us"*, and in John 14:23: *"If anyone loves Me, he will keep My word".* Two excellent meanings of "this" (as v. 3 begins) are provided by realizing that this section of 1John (4:7-5:3) describes love in our life-giving fellowship with God and His children: (1) this fellowship, and (2) 5:2's "we love God" and "observe [do] His commandments". Both parts of 5:2 are featured in this fellowship: John treats 1John receivers like they are <u>very aware</u> of it. Either (1) or (2) as "this" is a part of the love of God (A) that empowers us to keep all of His commandments. (<u>1John 5:3 explains</u> the key phrase in <u>John 15:9-10</u>: *"Stay in <u>My love</u>"* that includes keep My commandments comes from Father God's love).

5:16: If anyone sees his brother committing a sin not leading to death, he shall <u>ask</u> and God will for him give life to those who commit sin not leading to death. ᵇThere is a sin leading to death; I do not <u>say</u> **that** *[ina] he should <u>make request</u> for this.* In v. 16b, John still emphasizes v. 14's asking God <u>according to His will</u>: Vine under "ask" shows that *erōtaō* in v. 16b is a more presumptive asking than *aiteō* in v. 14-16a, where *aiteō* is used 4 times. "<u>That</u>" for *ina* in v. 16 <u>helps one assume</u> that "make request for this" identifies what John did not say. But he did not say billions of things, which veils <u>v. 16's content</u> that a <u>consistent (telic)</u> *ina* <u>brings out</u>: we do not ask presumptively, but ask according to His will (v. 14-16a). John did not say v. 14-16a <u>in order to</u> get a believer to ask presumptively (a <u>bad outcome</u>) for one who sins unto death.

5:21: *Little children, guard yourselves from idols.* I had regarded v. 21 as a surprising add-on ending of 1John until I saw v. 21's perfect fit for <u>1John's theme</u>: <u>stay (abide)</u> in <u>our life-giving fellowship with God in Jesus</u>. An idol is anything our hearts treasure so much that we may choose it over our life-giving fellowship in Jesus. Then idols are the key way believers are tempted to leave our 1John fellowship.

This section features 5 spiritually informative *ina*-verses and their contexts – 1John 3:1, 3:8, 3:11, 5:3, and 5:16 – whose *ina* <u>as</u> "<u>that</u>" can inform us wrongly, and which need explanations of outcomes and antecedent-sources that have rarely been considered. This lack of consideration is caused largely by translating *ina* as an <u>ambiguous</u> "<u>that</u>" <u>or</u> an <u>infinitive</u> (3:8), and by not realizing how fully God's call to the life-giving fellowship in 1:1-3 is in <u>all</u> of 1John.

The Consistently Telic Ina in 2John 5-6

2John 5-6 is the final Scripture where not translating *ina* as telic causes a vital loss of content (3John and Revelation are little affected).

⁵Now I ask you, lady, <u>not</u> as though I were writing to you [singular] a <u>new</u> <u>commandment</u>, but <u>the one</u> which we have <u>had from the beginning</u>, **that** *[ina] we love one another. ⁶And <u>this</u> is love,* **that** *[ina] we walk according to His commandments. This is the commandment, just as you [plural] have heard from the beginning, that [ina] you [plural] should walk in it. ⁷For [oti] ...* (2John 5-6, 7)

V. 5-6 show much evidence that the 2John receivers had the same "beginning of each one's life in Jesus" as 1John receivers (p. 40-42). As we discuss the content of v. 5-6, notice how the lady (v. 5) gets reminders like the initial 1John receivers. The "old-new command" in v. 5 is like 1John 2:7-8's "old-new command" (p. 35-37). V. 5's "reminder" is like 1John 3:11: *"¹¹For this is the message which you have heard from the beginning, that [ina] we should love one another."* Again (p. 40): "abide in Jesus" is a command (1John 2:7, 2:28, 3:23, 4:21; now 2John 5, 6), a message or precept (1John 3:11), and a word heard by "you" (1John 2:7; 2John 6). This command, message, or word, the one *"we have had from the beginning"* (v. 5; 2:7), is to set up *ina*'s outcome at the end of v. 5: we love one another (John 15:4-12, Chapters 1-5).

As v. 6 begins, "this" refers to "love one another" (as v. 5 ends) and / or to "love" (before the middle *ina*), and this *ina*'s outcome is our walk according to His commandments (plural, as in John 15:9-10). V. 6a is like 1John 5:3: *"³For this is the love of God, that [ina] we keep His commandments..."* 5:3 is also about our loving fellowship in Jesus (p. 46), 1John's singular command to stay in Him (1John 2:7-8, 2:28, 3:23, 4:21). 2John 5 and 6 each features a singular command, which is also the final *ina*'s source A for its outcome B: each should walk in IT (v. 6).

A consistent *ina* and singular command heard from the beginning help us realize that John gave brief reminders in both Epistles. We repeatedly find concise reminders in 1John to stay in Jesus, and now we see key content of 5 1John verses expressed even more concisely in 2John. V. 5-6 feature one command HEARD from the BEGINNING that should produce these outcomes: walking in IT and according to His commandments, and loving one another – all fitting very well with 1John 2:7, 3:11, 3:23, 4:21, and 5:3 (the five 1John verses).

1John's brief and 2John's briefer reminders can show us that the receivers of both Epistles were provided this key foundation to stay in Jesus that John's Gospel reveals. Clearly this foundation as we begin our life with Jesus can also equip believers today. We need to stay in the life-giving fellowship in Jesus with God and His children that John 15:1-17 and 1John describe. A telic *ina* in John 15, 1John, and 2John 5-6 all show that continuing in this loving fellowship (walk in it) should produce outcomes: loving one another and walking according to God's commandments (v. 5b-6a). This is like John 13:34's second A *ina* B, and also is like John 15:12-17, 1John 2:3-5 (God's love gets perfected in whoever keeps His word), and 1John 4:12 and 4:16-17 (p. 46): abiding in this loving fellowship causes love to be perfected in us.

I conclude that near the beginning of the lady's life in Jesus (and also those she was leading), she received many commands to keep (walk in) that were all included in the single command to "abide in Jesus" (His New Commandment), even like the 1John receivers.

John 15's "Abide in Jesus" Fellowship and the 1-2John Commandment

A telic *ina* helps us see evidence that initial 1John receivers had been GROUNDED in the life and fellowship that Jesus describes in John 15:1-17 (His New Commandment), so that they needed only to be reminded of this life and encouraged to stay in it. 2John 5-6 confirms all of this. Those only starting their life in Jesus were with those already in this full fellowship, who could clarify the brief reminders if needed by those starting in this fellowship. Let us review its key features.

As we saw on p. 22-27, John 15:1-17 emphasizes a fellowship with God through Jesus that includes 4 commands (v. 4, 7, 9, 17) plus His comprehensive statement in v. 10: "keep His commandments" is a key part of this abiding fellowship. Reconsider v. 9-10: *[9]Just as My Father has loved Me, I have also loved you; **abide in My love**. [10]If you **keep***

My commandments, you will abide in My love; just as I have kept My Father's commandments and abide in His love." As John 5:19, 30 and 1John 2:6 show (p. 6-7, 43-44), Jesus did nothing except what He heard and saw His Father doing, and one who says he abides in Jesus should walk as He walked. As Chapters 1-2 explain, abide (= stay) in Jesus' love is a special fellowship with Father God like Jesus had with Him while on earth: He gives us this opportunity for such a great life.

For 47 years I thought "stay in Jesus' love" is His easiest command to obey: He truly loves me so faithfully. Now I realize He tells us to stay in this fellowship: it is so special that we can easily move out of it. In 15:5 He warns, *"apart from Me you can do nothing"*, and 15:6 warns us about drying up. Sin can disrupt this fellowship (1John 3:4-9, p. 45), but Jesus can justly restore us into it (1John 1:9-2:2, p. 43-44).

This fellowship also includes commands for us to believe in the name of Jesus and to do all that He tells us, and especially features loving one another more effectively as an outcome of loving one another (John 13:34, 15:13-17, 1John 4:12-17, p. 22-23, p. 46). Jesus' command to stay in this fellowship is also in 15:4: *"Abide in Me, and I in you"*; or the shorter *"abide in Him"* in 1John 2:28. This is the singular "His commandment" and "His New Commandment" (1John 3:23, John 13:34, John 15:1-17) that John knew his initial receivers of 1John were grounded in (initial readers or hearers). 2John 5-6 shows evidence of this same foundation for the lady in v. 5.

John 15:1-17 refers explicitly to the 11 disciples' life with the Father and Jesus: our life with one another is really brought out in the outcome "loving one another" with John 17:20-26's extension to us. 1John 1:1-7 brings out our fellowship and life with one another far more than Jesus' words to the 11 disciples in John 15, and I believe this emphasis in 1John is one of its key additions to the rest of the Bible. This is affirmed by many verses throughout 1John referring to this key so smoothly.

Conclusions from John's Telic Ina in Major SIV's

You have seen 22 verses in which translating 25 *ina*'s as "so that" reveals a rarely seen theme and picture in John's Gospel and 1-2John. "Source A so that outcome B" generically provides *ina*'s telic meaning and brings out this Gospel-consistent theme in these 22 verses. *Ina*'s usual translations (23 "that" and 2 "to" in the NAS) can be a shortened "so that", but also can give no hint of the telic source A → outcome B. These 25 "possibly non-telic that's or to's" give apparent meanings that veil this theme to English readers and help translators stay ambiguous.

What is the key difference in the usual translations and this book's picture? Chapters 1-6 show that as a top long-term priority, we receive God as He draws us to connect to Him (or re-connect if this fits) and to stay with Him in the life-giving fellowship with Him and one another that He makes available to us in Jesus. Then God in us – the Source of our best love – will work with us and in us to increasingly produce essential outcomes of our close fellowship: we get to live more like Jesus, love one another and believe in Him better and increasingly, keep His commandments (obey all that He tells us), ask while abiding in Him, relationally get to know our Father and Jesus better and better...

Here is a broad overview of what I see about this unveiled theme:

* John 1-6 is a partial unveiling of the unseen Source in Jesus' life on earth and the first hint of His calling us disciples to the same kind of life and fellowship with Father God through our *Logos* Word, Jesus (p. 5-17 show key features of this).

* John 7-12 is a time of incubation with this partial insight, during which we can see more of invisible Father God's work in Jesus' life. {In John 10, we can also see further partial insight given to those who could receive it. Jesus says that He is the only Door for the sheep (v. 7-9) and is the Good Shepherd and one with His Almighty Father (v. 11, 27-30). Relating to John's unveiled theme, Jesus as the only Door is a new hint of our first need: to truly connect with Father God through Jesus. Jesus as the Good Shepherd who is one with His Almighty Father shows His total ability to keep others from taking His sheep out of our special fellowship with Him (to fulfill His role in protecting it). In John 10:38, believing Jesus' works can help produce *ina*'s

outcome: the Jews and we readers come to know and understand that Jesus had <u>the special John 14:20, 15:4-10 fellowship</u> with His Father (p. 130).}

* John 13-17 provided the full disclosure of this life and fellowship to the 11 disciples, and John 17:20-23 explicitly extends it to believers in Jesus through their word.

* John 18-21 shows Jesus' ultimate example of "greater love no one has" in John 15:12-13. John 18-19 shows how much He was willing to suffer in order to provide good for us. John 20-21 shows Jesus' loving interaction with His followers and disciples in His resurrected life. This helps believers today because John 1-19 shows interactions with His people only before His resurrection, but today we interact with the risen Lord Jesus, and the glimpses we see in John 20-21 confirm that His wonderful love continues.

* 1John and 2John can show this fellowship and life to be a key part of the foundation of those who initially received these Epistles. Many brief reminders of this abiding fellowship with its outworkings provide evidence that initial receivers of these two Epistles knew well this John 15 fellowship with its outworkings. I consider this to be evidence that new believers today should have this same kind of foundation.

You can see a simple picture that I find fits all 22 verses better than we usually see. This is a key find: a Biblically-sound, Gospel-consistent telic meaning for <u>all</u> of John's *ina*'s that <u>his initial readers or hearers</u> (receivers) could realize without a deep analysis <u>confirms each telic *ina*</u>, <u>reveals a key theme of John and vital source-outcome relationships</u> for our lives, and is a major start to seeing that John did not use *ina* in this unusual way that is usually assumed.

{   But we must do a deep analysis today. Why? Assuming that John <u>sometimes</u> used "*ina* B" to identify an unidentified word in A (like "*oti* B" does) provides <u>different apparent meanings</u> to <u>a purely telic *ina*</u> in some verses. But you can see a great loss of content in all 22 verses, and see NO REAL NEED TO ASSUME he used *ina* <u>in these verses</u> unlike his normally telic *ina*.   }

Chapters 1-6 (which essentially duplicate the shorter book, *Stay in My Love*) have emphasized the major content that normally is not seen in John's writings. Part 2 (Chapter 7 onward) can help us see explicitly the ways John did use *ina* and *oti*, so that we can know the truth.

Part 2

What Is God's and John's True Meaning of *Ina*?

Chapters 1-6 should show us that IF John consistently used *ina* to connect a source or start A to its projected end or outcome B, then we find a vital Biblical picture normally not seen in English translations of John's Gospel and 1John and 2John. Consider the content shown in Chapters 1-6 that the telic *ina* adds to the usual understanding of John's Gospel and 1John. Each telic *ina* adds its useful insight to the whole picture that probably is new to us.

How can we know which is John's true meaning of *ina*? Part 2 with Apx. 1-3 is a Bible study written for anyone to check my statements and evidence about his meaning of *ina*. We can see all 213 of John's *ina*'s with good antecedent-sources and outcomes for initial readers in order to know how consistently he used a telic *ina* (Chapter 8); see that the *ina* as if *oti* assumption is truly not needed in John's Scriptures (Chapter 8); see how he used *oti*, including often to identify an unidentified word in A (Chapter 7: as you saw, the usual source of conflict in SIV's); see key ways that he carefully distinguished *ina* and *oti* (Chapter 7, Apx. 3); and see more of how "using *ina* as if it were *oti* to identify A" can add a major complication (Apx. 4) and loss of content to other *ina*-verses in John's Scriptures (Chapters 1-6 show a huge loss of content in John's SIV's).

Chapter 7 should be regarded as a part of the book to be read by those who want or need to see more to confirm or correct the basis for this unveiled theme or picture in John's Gospel, 1John, and 2John. Chapter 8 and Apx. 1-3 are arranged in an order so that a reader can find a topic that he or she wants to see – like an encyclopedia and unlike the sequential Chapters 1-7. Chapter 8 shows a "telic A-B source-outcome relationship" for every ina in John's Scriptures, so that Chapter 8 as a unit can reveal what he means with ina, or you may prefer to read only verses where a telic ina is not obvious to you.

Each section in Apx. 1-3 is more elective for each reader. Each section can be good and needed for some readers and not useful now for many other readers. Those interested may request Apx. 4.

Apx. 1 shows four complete groups of John's ina's. Each group can be useful for some readers, but I call attention to section 3: there I put into a group every ina-verse for which I anticipate it may be hard to identify a good source A or a relevant outcome B of this source.

Apx. 2 shows my judgment for the meaning of each of John's 413 oti's and shows how John used oti in two complete groups of his oti-verses. This gives 61 examples (in addition to 36 in Chapter 7) of his use of oti.

Apx. 3 shows 3 comparisons of complete groups of John's ina's to show John's clear and consistent distinction in using ina and oti with each conjunction's distinct meanings. I compare his use of ina and oti using complete groups of these conjunctions, so that you can know that I do not pick out examples in order to "pseudo-prove my point". Apx. 3 ends with showing a source-outcome telic meaning of ina in Matt. 5:29 (p. 17). It was Marshall's chosen example to illustrate how New Testament writers sometimes used ina with a non-telic meaning, but Matt. 5:29 also allows a consistently telic ina.

Apx. 4 shows that IF John often used ina with a non-telic meaning (at least 15 out of 213 ina's), then this would remove Scriptural authority in source-outcome content whenever he used ina. Apx. 4 is not included in this book because Apx. 4 assumes a non-telic ina to show how bad that assumption is: this could confuse especially readers who flip through the book. I recommend Apx. 4 only to those who want or need my evidence of John's purely telic ina beyond what I give in this book. I intend to email Apx. 4 for free if you ask at jamesmtarter@aol.com.

Chapter 7

John's *Ina* and John's *Oti*

In Chapter 7 we shall see that a further examination of a possibly non-telic *ina* reveals severe problems with it, which makes it is a poor and totally unneeded solution for unreal problems in about 30 verses. Here I offer two causes beyond Chapters 1-6 and 8 for concluding that John used a purely telic *ina* (p. 17-20): one is his consistent use of *ina* with a contingent verb in B (p. 56-57). The second is realizing how John used *oti*, so that we realize how bad it is to assume that he meant *oti* when he actually wrote *ina*. Briefly, I find much evidence (p. 57-68) that John did not use *ina* as if it were *oti*.

An Infinitive Often Losing the Telic Ina: Jesus' Food in John 4:34

All English translations I have seen agree with the NAS on the key idea in John 4:34, claiming that Jesus said: *"My food is to do the will of Him who sent Me and to accomplish His work"* (NAS). You know how you have normally read the infinitive "to do" in v. 34: both "to do" and the gerund "doing" (in some translations) act as a noun that identifies Jesus' food, with the "to" providing no telic meaning at all. This is a feature of any "to-verb": unless the context shows a telic "to", "to-verb" is read as a totally non-telic infinitive. In the two translations I checked, ALL 54 of John's *ina*'s that the NAS translated as "to" are infinitives, and ALL 35 of John's *ina*'s the KJV translated as "to" are infinitives. The Greek *ina* is normally telic, but the common English translation "to-verb" by itself does not contain a telic meaning. Consider this in 4:34.

On p. 12-16 we saw that Jesus ate His special food (to hear God and see His work in His special fellowship with Him), and it equipped Him to do His Father's will and work. We also saw that Jesus did not identify His food in the close context, but in the larger context of John 4-15. This whole picture in John that is communicated by *ina*'s normal telic meaning is totally missed in English translations of 4:34.

John Showing B's Contingency by His Consistently Subjunctive Verb

1John 3:8 (p. 45) illustrates a big change in content if we simplify an *ina* subjunctive to an infinitive: "*[8]...The Son of God appeared for this purpose, to [ina] destroy the works of the devil."* "To destroy" is normally read as if "to destroy the works of the devil" is "this purpose" – identifying it. "To destroy" comes from *ina luse*, which is subjunctive aorist and not indicative or infinitive or any other *luo*. This subjunctive contains a contingency (a "maybe not") fitting for a telic outcome but not for identifying "this purpose". (John 4:34's change [p. 12] is similar).

1John 3:8 shows our need to know a little Greek in order to confirm the truth in this section. The Greek subjunctive mood has a special function: to express that its idea is not yet a fact, but is an "if" (a maybe not) contingent on its fulfillment. Here are basic facts from a Greek scholar writing without 3:8 or this issue in mind. I quote from Zodhiates' *Key Word Study Bible* (grammatical definitions #) plus {Wikipedia}:

The Subjunctive Mood makes an assertion about which there is some doubt, uncertainty, or indefiniteness. It is closely related to the future tense, which helps point up the fact that often the uncertainty only arises because the action has not yet occurred. (# 43)

The subjunctive mood is specifically distinguished from the indicative mood ("The *Indicative Mood* makes an assertion of fact": Zodhiates # 24) and from the imperative ("The *Present Imperative* is a command to do something in the future and involves continuous or repeated action": Zodhiates # 37).

{The optative mood was used to express wish or potentiality, but was increasingly replaced by the subjunctive, and in the New Testament was primarily used in set phrases (Wikipedia). I did not notice John using an optative in any *ina*-verse: this leaves us with the factual indicative (especially present tense), contingent subjunctive, and commanding imperative.}

Here is the <u>key point</u> in this section: in John's Gospel and 3 Epistles <u>John consistently used</u> a <u>contingent verb after</u> *ina* and a <u>factual indicative verb after</u> *oti*. *Ina*'s contingent verbs <u>confirm</u>: <u>John decisively treated *ina* and *oti* differently</u> (the next topic, p. 57-68) and <u>support</u> *ina* <u>B as a telic OUTCOME</u> in contrast to <u>a present fact</u>. P. 108-114 show: a few "complications" do not affect this conclusion (a future indicative might be a fact only in the future – not now – and an *oti* statement itself may be contingent [as with the "if" in 1John 1:6 on p. 58]…).

Reminders of Basic Features of a Telic Ina for Comparing It With Oti

In this section I point out key features of John's *ina* (shown on p. 17-20) in order to better examine *ina* vs. *oti*:

* Conjunctions *ina* and *oti* are both normally written as A *ina* B or A *oti* B (no exception to either form changes content or the A-B relationship: p. 99-100, 124-126);

* To simplify writing, unless otherwise indicated I call telic *ina*'s A "the source" (a source or start), and call B "the outcome" (a possible or projected or desired outcome, result, end, or extent). <u>Telic</u> connects a projected outcome to its source and shows their relationship;

* In *ina*'s A → B, the arrow shows that a "source A" might cause (or help cause), lead to, produce, precede, project to, extend to, or result in *ina*'s "outcome B";

* If a source-outcome relationship between A and B is clear, the often non-telic words "that" or "to" may also be a clear translation of a telic *ina* (because the telic A-B relationship is often clear or no big issue);

* If John is <u>informing</u> the reader about a <u>less obvious</u> source-outcome relationship, non-telic meanings of "that" and "to" force us to add words (like "so that", "in order that", "in order to"…), or else an <u>English reader is naturally helped to assume</u> that *ina*'s A-B relationship is <u>non-telic</u>.

John's Use of Oti B to Identify A

John used *oti* B 234 times to <u>identify</u> A (57% of his 413 *oti*'s). John also used *oti* 179 times (the other 43%) to show "A because B": B shows "why A", a <u>relationship of A to B</u> that goes in a different direction

(A ← B) from *ina's normally telic direction* (A → B). We shall further discuss the *oti* = because later (especially p. 61-64).

Did you notice in the key verses in Chapters 1-6 (or on p. 59) that major translations use *ina* to identify A instead of show "why A"? John uses *oti* B to identify, further identify, or clarify the meaning of A: a way to write "A, specifically B". In A *oti* B, A identifies a BIG CATEGORY, and B IDENTIFIES the SPECIFIC ITEM WITHIN this big category. Let us first see clear examples of how John used *oti* B to identify its A, and then we can compare this with how he used A *ina* B (p. 59-61).

John 1:34: *"I myself have seen, and have testified that [oti] this is the Son of God."* "This is the Son of God" B identifies what John the Baptist had seen and testified out of all he had seen and testified A.

John 5:42: *"But I know you, that [oti] you do not have the love of God in yourselves."* Here Jesus identifies the specific feature that He knew concerning them out of all He knew concerning them.

John 7:35: *"...Where does this man intend to go that [oti] we will not find Him?..."* B (a place specifically where they would not find Jesus) clarifies or identifies the kind of place in A (A effectively asked, where is a place He will go?).

John 9:8: *Therefore the neighbors, and those who previously saw him as [oti, that he was] a beggar, were saying...* B identifies specifically what they saw when they previously saw him out of everything else they saw when looking at him (A).

John 11:27: *"Yes, Lord; I have believed that [oti] You are the Christ, the Son of God, even He who comes into the world."* B identifies specifically what Martha believed out of all she believed.

John 19:35: *And he who has seen has testified, and his testimony is true; and he knows that [oti] he is telling the truth, so that [ina] you also may believe.* Oti's B (John is telling the truth) specifically identifies what John knew out of all John knew. {"His testimony is true" can also be in a larger A. And also, v. 35's *ina* is clearly telic.}

1John 1:6: *If we say that [oti] we have fellowship with Him [end of B] and yet walk in the darkness, we lie and do not practice the truth.* "B" in 1:6 (and 1:8, 10 quoted on p. 139) identifies what we could say (the "if" in 1:6, 8, 10 causes my contingent "could"), and none of the 3 *oti* B's is *ina's* projected outcome of what we could say.

Rev. 3:1: *"I know your deeds,* **that** *[oti] you have a name* **that** *[oti] you are alive, but you are dead."* All of v. 1 after the first *oti* is its B that, <u>out of all that Jesus knew</u> about the Church in Sardis' deeds, <u>identifies</u> the <u>key feature</u> Jesus knew about this church's deeds and it (A): dead deeds from being dead despite its name. The second *oti*'s "you are alive" is its B that <u>identifies</u> its A – identifies the <u>kind of name</u> this church had out of all kinds of names it could have had.

Notice how translations normally assume *ina* B identifies A like *oti* B in major <u>SIV's</u> (<u>Spiritually Informative Verses</u>) in John's Scriptures:

* John 4:34 (p. 12-13): "Doing His Father's will" is assumed to identify Jesus' <u>unknown</u> food (v. 32) out of all kinds of food that He also ate.

* John 6:29 (p. 15-17): "Believe in Jesus" is assumed to identify the work of God out of all kinds of work for followers of Jesus.

* John 13:34, 15:12, 15:17 (p. 21-27): "Love one another" is assumed to identify Jesus' new commandment, "My commandment", and what He commands in v. 17 out of all of His possible commandments.

* 1John 3:23 (p. 37-38): Both "believe in Jesus" and "love one another" are assumed to identify "His [God's] commandment" (singular).

* 1John 4:21 (p. 38-39): "God-lover, love your brother also" is assumed to identify "this commandment" out of all possible commands.

* 2John 5-6 (p. 47-49): Three *ina*'s in two verses where each *ina* B is assumed to identify its A (like the previous examples in this list).

In most of John's uses of *oti* to identify A, the <u>verb itself</u> <u>is</u> the <u>A</u> (in 201 *oti*'s out of John's 234 *oti* B's to identify A), and B identifies the <u>specific action</u> of a <u>verb</u> in A. John 1:34, 11:27, 19:35, and 1John 1:6 in the above examples illustrate this group of almost half of John's 413 *oti*'s. But *oti* <u>clearly identifies</u> <u>only</u> <u>its verb</u> in nearly all of these 201 *oti*'s (not 19:35): few are like the SIV's that need comparing.

Having seen how John used *oti* B to identify A, we are now ready to make a <u>strong direct comparison of *ina* and *oti*</u> to see <u>their difference in SIV's</u> (spiritually informative verses): <u>John often used *oti* B to identify a word in A without an antecedent</u> (a word in *oti*'s A that is not clearly identified in the text before that word). Chapter 8 shows that <u>no *ina* B</u>

is <u>needed</u> to identify a word in its A, and Chapters 1-8 or p. 101-107 in Apx. 1 explain how a <u>telic *ina*</u> can work <u>in every *ina*</u> B that I often see <u>translated to read as if</u> it identifies A like *oti* B does (usually that or to). <u>Now</u> <u>we consider *oti*</u>: the following verses illustrate how John used *oti* B to <u>identify or clarify</u> an <u>unidentified or vague</u> word or idea <u>in A</u>.

John 8:47: ^a*He who is of God hears the words of God;* ^b*for <u>this reason</u> you do not hear them,* **because** [*oti*] *you are not of God.* This is an "*oti* = because" verse on p. 62, but *oti* B <u>identifies</u> a <u>vague</u> "this reason": 8:45-46 is about not believing Jesus and v. 47a is only about <u>hearing</u> God, but B in v. 47b identifies "<u>this reason</u> you do <u>not</u> <u>hear</u>" (*oti*'s A).

John 9:30: ...*Well, <u>here</u> is <u>an amazing thing</u>,* **that** [*oti*] *you do not know where He is from, and yet He opened my eyes.* B (their not knowing about this miraculous man Jesus) <u>specifically identifies</u> what the formerly blind man called an amazing thing in A, and nothing before v. 30 showed what he would call "here" (lit., "in this") or an amazing thing.

John 21:22-23: ²²*Jesus said to him, "If I want him to remain until I come, what is that to you? You follow Me!"* ²³*Therefore <u>this saying</u> went out among the brethren* **that** [*oti*] *that disciple would not die....* B (that disciple would not die) <u>specifically identifies</u> "this saying" in A. You can see that "this saying" was identified by the B that came after A *oti* and not identified by an antecedent in v. 22 (and you could also see that nothing before v. 22 identifies "this saying = John would not die").

1John 1:5: *And <u>this</u> is <u>the message we have heard from Him and announce to you</u>,* **that** [*oti*] <u>*God is light*</u>, *and in Him there is no darkness at all.* "God is light and has no darkness in Him" (B) <u>identifies</u> "this" and "the message we heard from Him and announce to you" (A). 1:1-4 does not identify "this" or the message B (God is light, and...).

1John 2:2-3: ²*and He Himself is the propitiation for our sins; and not for ours only, but also for those of the whole world.* ³<u>*By this*</u> *we <u>know</u>* **that** [*oti*] *we have come to know Him, <u>if we keep His commandments</u>.* V. 3 after *oti* <u>identifies</u> both "this" (<u>*if we keep...*</u>) and "what we know" (*have come to <u>know Him if we keep...</u>*) out of all we know. (I quote v. 2 to help you see that neither is identified before v. 3).

1John 3:1: ^{1a}....^b*For <u>this reason</u> the world does not know us,* **because** [*oti*] *it did <u>not know Him</u>.* Oti B <u>identifies</u> "this reason" the world does <u>not know us</u> after v. 1a is about God's loving us (like John 8:47 above).

1John 3:15-16: ¹⁵*Everyone who hates his brother is a murderer; and you know that no murderer has eternal life abiding in him.* ¹⁶*We <u>know</u>*

love by *this*, **that** [*oti*] *He laid down His life for us; and we ought to lay down our lives for the brethren.* Jesus' laying down His life for us is the B that identifies "this" and how we know love (A). Neither is identified by an antecedent, as v. 15 shows (v. 12-14 are negatives like v. 15 instead of a way we know love).

Rev. 2:5-6: [5]*Therefore remember from where you have fallen, and repent and do the deeds you did at first; or else I am coming to you and will remove your lampstand out of its place – unless you repent.* [6]*Yet* this *you do* have, **that** [*oti*] *you hate the deeds of the Nicolaitans, which I also hate.* Hating the deeds of the Nicolaitans (B) specifically identifies a good "this" that the church did have. B contrasts with their issue for repentance in v. 4-5, so you can see that the good "this you do have" in v. 6 does not have an identifying antecedent.

Rev. 2:13-16: [13]*I know where you dwell, where Satan's throne is; and you* hold fast My name, *and did* not deny My faith *even in the days of Antipas, My witness, My faithful one, who was killed among you, where Satan dwells.* [14]*But* I have *a* few things against *you,* [b]**because** [*oti*] *you have there some who hold the teaching of Balaam, who kept teaching Balak to put a stumbling block before the sons of Israel, to eat things sacrificed to idols and to commit acts of immorality.* [15]*So you also have some who in the same way hold the teaching of the Nicolaitans.* [16]*Therefore repent ....* "Because" is a valid translation of *oti* in v. 14, but *oti* B (v. 14b-15) clearly identifies a "few things" and probably is Jesus' point more than showing why He had them against them. You can see from Jesus' commendation in v. 13 (or before if you look) that no antecedent identifies the "few things" that Jesus had against them.

I regard the above 9 examples of John using *oti* B to identify an underlined word in A as easy to see: easy to eliminate other ways to identify the word. Because John often used *oti* B to identify A, would he stop using *oti* and use an abnormal meaning of *ina* to inform us about a major topic? If you cannot answer "no" now, then you should realize that a careful writer would not use *ina* like *oti*, and I see much more evidence that God and John are very careful in their use.

Oti May Reverse the Telic Ina's Source-Outcome Relationship

"Causes" are one kind of source. *Ina* and *oti* are both conjunctions, but may have incompatible meanings. In 179 of John's 413 A *oti* B's

(43%, safely 41% to 46%), B shows why A (= because or a causal for).
Oti = because is an "outcome A – cause or source B" that may reverse
the telic ina's A → B. As I wrote A → B to show the A-B relationship in
A ina B (p. 19 or 57), A ← B shows A oti B's reverse A-B outcome-
cause (source) relationship: in A because B, A is an outcome and B a
major cause, reason, or source. These 4 oti's clearly show how A oti B
can reverse ina's telic source A → outcome B in A ina B.

John 3:18: *He who believes in Him is not judged; he who does not
believe has been judged already,* **because** *[oti] he has not believed in
the name of the only begotten Son of God.* Oti's B (not believing in the
name of Jesus) is a source or cause of this outcome: one being judged
already (A ← B). Ina's A → B would deny God's justice in His judging
each person: God's judging is not a source A of deadly unbelief (B).

John 8:37: *I know that [oti] you are Abraham's descendants; yet you
seek to kill Me,* **because** *[oti] My word has no place in you.* The bold
oti B explains why they sought to kill Jesus: His word having no place
in them CAUSED them to seek to kill Him (A ← B). 8:40 (they sought
to kill Jesus who gave God's truth) confirms B as a source and not an
outcome, so this is definitely not ina's A → B. [Being Abraham's
descendants is the first oti's B that specifically identifies what Jesus
knew about them out of all that Jesus knew: no A - B arrow for this oti.]

John 8:47: [a]*He who is of God hears the words of God;* [b]*for this reason
you do not hear them,* **because** *[oti] you are not of God.* A solution of
a problem fixes its source. If I never hear God (oti's outcome A), then I
need to truly connect with Jesus so that I will be of God: this corrects
the bad source B with John's unveiled theme. V. 47a confirms this
solution to v. 47b's A ← B: *"He who is of God hears the words of God"*.

1John 4:19: *We love,* **because** *[oti] He first loved us.* If we are not
loving long-term as we should, then how do we start loving better? Is
"we love" a source or an outcome? Both v. 19's oti and "first" in its B
clearly show that "He first loved us" is a SOURCE or cause of our love
and must be fixed for a long-term solution. (Here I add that my realizing
God's love for unworthy me equips me to love unworthy others). A ← B

You may check that in all 4 oti = because statements above, a telic
ina (so that) instead of oti would reverse the relationship of A with B
and greatly change the content of each verse (I did the first 2 for you).

We see *oti* = because (A ← B) can show a <u>reverse source-outcome relationship</u> from a telic *ina* (A → B). This displays the <u>grave danger</u> of treating *ina* as if it were *oti* in a <u>spiritually informative verse</u> (SIV) that <u>informs us</u> about <u>the relationship of a source and its outcome</u>: *ina* <u>cannot show with authority</u> a source-outcome relationship <u>from any *ina*-verse in John</u> <u>IF</u> he did not normally distinguish *ina* from *oti*.

I find that he did, but major translations ASSUME that he did not. John <u>could not</u> use *ina* when he meant *oti* in 20 to 40 SIV's without <u>destroying the full authority in</u> the <u>content of the A → B relationship</u> in <u>all of</u> his 213 *ina's*.

I illustrate how this "*ina* as if it were *oti*" assumption can remove authoritative content from every *ina* verse: imagine if John wrote "red" for a "blue" color 30 times spread out in his 213 times of writing "red", and he also wrote "blue" 413 other times to mean "blue" or "violet". In this case, what does "red" mean in any <u>1</u> of his 213 uses?

I find that <u>neither John nor God's Spirit</u> removed the authoritative content of the often-informative <u>source-outcome relationship</u> in <u>all of</u> John's 213 *ina*-statements. You can judge that in Chapter 8.

In this paragraph I report on another <u>big</u> conclusion that <u>John clearly and consistently demonstrated</u> in his <u>179 *oti* = because (A ← B) statements</u>. Of 179 *oti's*, I find over 140 in which <u>A as the outcome</u> or <u>B as the source</u> seems very clearly specified by the context or situation or sequence; far fewer that are not as clear; about 25 in which either A or B could be the cause (without further analysis); and <u>zero</u> (none) that flows <u>like a telic *ina*</u>: in the telic *ina's* A → B, <u>A</u> is <u>a source of an</u> "outcome" <u>B</u>. 140+ to 0 in the <u>very clear uses</u> is utterly <u>consistent</u>! I identify every judgment-call in Apx. 2 (but I do not quote the *oti*-verses in Apx. 2: I expect "few" readers would read explanations about 179 *oti's*, but every reader should be able to <u>check what I report to you</u>).

So far I believe that I have shown: a good way with confirmations for every *ina* we have seen in John to be telic (Chapters 1-6, and every *ina* by John is in Chapter 8); a resulting picture in John's Gospel and 1-2John that can show how much vital, Biblically-sound content is lost in major translations of these books; John often using *oti* B to identify unidentified or vague A words like "this" (p. 60-61); and two ways (a huge loss of source-outcome content and putting an <u>unnecessary and sometimes reversed</u> meaning on the normal *ina*) to <u>see how bad it is to assume</u> that John used *ina* about 30 times when he meant *oti*. From this discussion plus Chapter 8, I conclude: John did not use *ina* like *oti*.

But like me, you form your opinions before God, and you may still believe that many of the usual non-telic *ina*-verse translations are better than a purely telic *ina* translation. There is more to see of <u>how John was far more careful in his use of *ina* and *oti*</u> than the major translations of SIV's clearly assume, and how a non-telic *ina* in major translations is <u>a worse option than is normally considered</u>. The evidence gets longer (more thorough and not as convincing by itself), but <u>adds</u> <u>to the above</u> to help us see more and more that John was too careful in his use of *ina* and *oti* to mix them up in his SIV's (spiritually informative *ina*-verses). I encourage you to read only as much as you need or want after this section so that you can <u>form a right conclusion</u> about John's use of a purely telic *ina*.

John's Careful and Consistent Use of Ina and Oti Differently

Seeing that John distinguished *ina* and *oti* <u>carefully and consistently</u> can help you "<u>know</u>" that he would not write *ina* as if it were *oti* in crucially important SIV's. In this section we see how carefully and consistently <u>John used both *ina* and *oti*</u> in <u>their distinct ways</u> within 15 different Scriptural contexts. In Apx. 3 (p. 128-139), we can see that these 15 contexts are representative of <u>all contexts</u> where John used *ina* and *oti* in <u>one verse</u> <u>plus 3</u> <u>2-verse-units</u> (45 contexts).

We can see that John consistently used *ina* B with its A → B telic meaning, and *oti* B with either of its usual meanings: "identify A" (with its "no arrow"), or "show why A" in an "*oti*=because" A ← B.

John 3:21: *But he who practices the truth comes to the Light, **so that** [ina] his deeds may be manifested ᵇas [oti] having been wrought in God.* Having been wrought in God (*oti*'s B) identifies what his deeds manifest (*oti*'s A). Being wrought in God also causes the deeds to manifest their Source: *oti*=because's A ← B (both meanings of *oti* fit v. 21). In a larger A for *oti*, v. 20-21a, *oti*'s B causes some to come to the Light. In contrast, coming to the Light (*ina*'s A) sets up this possible outcome: his deeds are manifested as wrought in God. *Ina*'s A → B.

John 5:36: *But the testimony which I have is greater than the testimony of John; for the works which the Father has given Me **to** [ina] accomplish – the very works that I do – testify about Me, **that** [oti] the Father has sent Me.* "The Father sent Jesus" is *oti*'s B that identifies what was testified (*oti*'s A). The Father gave Jesus works (*ina*'s A) so that Jesus should do and accomplish them (*ina*'s intended outcome B: *ina*'s A → B). After being given each work, Jesus did it, and its specific testimony about Him was *oti* the Father sent Jesus.

John 6:5: *Therefore Jesus, lifting up His eyes and seeing **that** [oti] a large crowd was coming to Him, said to Philip, "Where are we to buy bread, **so that** [ina] these may eat?"* "A large crowd coming to Jesus" (*oti*'s B) identifies specifically (specifies) what Jesus saw (*oti*'s A) out of all He saw. (Notice that a telic *ina* B – so that – cannot replace *oti* B in v. 5). Buying bread (*ina*'s A) would set up this desired outcome: people eat (*ina*'s A → B). ("People eating" is not a specific "buying bread", unlike *oti*'s meaning of identifying a specific A.)

John 7:23: *If a man receives circumcision on the Sabbath **so that** [ina] the Law of Moses will not be broken, are you angry with Me **because** [oti] I made an entire man well on the Sabbath?* Jesus asked those Jews who were rejecting Him: Is "I made an entire man well on the Sabbath" (*oti*'s B) the real cause of their anger (*oti*'s A ← B)? *Ina*'s telic A → B is also clear: they provided circumcision on the Sabbath (*ina*'s source A) in order to produce *ina*'s intended outcome B: not break the Law of Moses.

John 9:22: *His parents said this **because** [oti] they were afraid of the Jews; for the Jews had already agreed **that** [ina] if anyone confessed Him to be Christ, he was to be put out of the synagogue.* Being afraid of the Jews shows why his parents said "this (= v. 20-21)": *oti*'s A ← B. *Ina*'s B (9:22 after *ina*) logically could be either the intended outcome from the agreement (*ina*'s A → B) or identifying what was agreed. A telic *ina* in v. 22 shows John's insight that their agreement was for an intended outcome: to intimidate any person out of confessing Christ or to punish anyone who did. A telic *ina* displays their stealthy purpose in what they agreed: this shows how a telic *ina* adds an insight with an authority that may be lost if *ina* is sometimes non-telic (which "that" is).

John 14:31: *but so that [ina] the world may know that [oti] I love the Father, I do exactly as the Father commanded Me....* Jesus' love for His Father (*oti*'s B) identifies specifically what the world is to come to know (*oti*'s A) – as usual for *oti*. *Ina* in v. 31 is an "*ina* B A" statement: p. 99-100 show that writing *ina* B before A never affects John's telic meaning of *ina*, and v. 31 illustrates this fact. The content and source-outcome relationship of A with B is not changed if Jesus had said, "I do exactly as the Father commanded Me (A) so that the world may know that I love the Father (B)". This is A *ina* B with the same source and outcome as the Scripture: *ina*'s A → B.

John 16:4: *But these things I have spoken to you, so that [ina] when their hour comes, you may remember that [oti] I told you of them. These things I did not say to you at the beginning, because [oti] I was with you.* V. 4 in the NAS shows all 3 key translations: a telic *ina* and *oti* with its 2 meanings. The first *oti*'s B identifies specifically what the disciples were to remember: Jesus had told them of these things. The second *oti* B shows why Jesus did not tell them these things at the beginning: "I was with you" (cause B of this *oti*'s outcome A in A ← B). In contrast to these two meanings of *oti* in John's writings, v. 4's *ina* is telic. Jesus spoke these things (*ina*'s source A) in order to set up *ina*'s outcome B: the disciples would remember that He told them these things when their hour of fulfillment did come (*ina*'s B in *ina*'s A → B).

John 16:32: *Behold, an hour is coming, and has already come, for [ina] you to be scattered, each to his own home, and to leave Me alone; and yet I am not alone, because [oti] the Father is with Me.* The Father being with Jesus (*oti*'s B) shows why He was not alone (*oti*'s A): A ← B. *Ina* again is the telic A → B: "an hour has already come" would quickly get an outcome prophesied for it: the disciples get scattered.

John 17:20-21: *I do not ask on behalf of these alone, but for those also who believe in Me through their word; [21]that [ina] they may all be one; even as You, Father, are in Me and I in You, [b]that [ina] they also may be in Us, so that [ina] the world may believe that [oti] You sent Me.* You sent Me (*oti*'s B) identifies what the world should believe. Jesus' prayer in v. 20 is a source for the first *ina*'s B: an outcome of our being one as Jesus and the Father are one, or like the 11 being one in 17:11.

This A and B are the next *ina*'s A: its B outcome is our being "in Them" (in the special fellowship in John 15:4-10, 14:20). This B with v. 20-21a is the third *ina*'s A: our being "in God" sets up its outcome, the world believes *oti* Father God sent Jesus (this *ina*'s B). All *ina*'s are A → B.

John 17:24: *Father, I desire **that** [ina] they also, whom You have given Me, be with Me where I am, **so that** [ina] they may see My glory which You have given Me, **for** [oti] You loved Me before the foundation of the world.* The first *ina* illustrates a special feature of *ina* with verbs like desire, ask, agree, and plan. These verbs are often followed by *ina* to show the intended goal or outcome of what was desired, asked... If *oti* followed any of these verbs, this would usually identify the specific desire, request... Often a specific action and its goal are the same (as in v. 24), but if *oti* and *ina* keep their distinct meanings, then an insight is added and a misleading impression avoided by a telic *ina* or an *oti*: John 9:22 (p. 65-66), or 11:53, 57 and 12:10 (p. 79-80) are examples.

With the second *ina*, being with Jesus where He is (A) sets up our seeing His glory (a projected outcome B; *ina*'s A → B). *Oti* shows the same outcome from the opposite direction (*oti*'s A ← B): the Father's love for Jesus before the foundation of the world (*oti*'s B) is a source of Jesus' glory that preceded the disciples seeing it (*oti*'s A). In v. 24, "see My glory" is the outcome (*ina*'s B and *oti*'s A) with both conjunctions placed to show this relationship: "A *ina* B *oti*=because C", or A → B ← C, with 1 outcome B of its sources A and C. { An "*ina-oti*-sandwich" like this is in 1John 4:17 (p. 46, 137) and 2John 6-7 (p. 138), but *oti* was not a topic before Chapter 7. John 11:15 (p. 100, 130) and 1John 3:10-11 (p. 136) are 2 reversed *ina-oti* sandwiches: 2 outcomes come from 1 source, outcome-A *oti*=because source-B *ina* outcome-C, or A ← B → C. All 5 *ina-oti* sandwiches display John's distinct *ina-oti* use. }

John 18:8-9: *Jesus answered, "I told you **that** [oti] I am He; so if you seek Me, let these go their way," [9]**to** [ina] fulfill the word which He spoke, "[oti] Of those whom You have given Me I lost not one."* "I am" is the first *oti*'s B that identifies specifically what Jesus told them. The [untranslated second] *oti* B identifies specifically what Jesus spoke. An expanded literal translation of the "*ina* B = to B" is "so that the word would be fulfilled...". Jesus' command, "let these go", led to *ina*'s outcome B: fulfilling His word, "...I lost not one" (a telic A *ina* B: A → B).

1John 2:19: *They went out from us, but they were not really of us; for if they had been of us, they would have remained with us; but they went out, **so that** [ina] it would be shown **that** [oti] they all are not of us.* "They all are not of us" (*oti*'s B) identifies what was shown by their going out (*oti*'s A: v. 19 up to *oti*). *Ina*'s A (the leavers' going out from John's group) produced its outcome B: showing openly (manifesting) that they were <u>not of</u> John's group (true disciples). *Ina's A → B*

1John 3:5: *You <u>know</u> **that** [oti] He <u>appeared</u> **in order to** [**ina**] take away sins; and in Him there is no sin.* "He appeared in order to take away sins" (*oti's* B) <u>identifies specifically</u> what "you know" (*oti's* A) out of all you know. Taking away sins is *ina's* B and is a major intended outcome of Jesus appearing on earth (*ina's* source A). *Ina's A → B*

1John 4:9: *By <u>this</u> the <u>love of God</u> was <u>manifested</u> <u>in us</u>, **that** [oti] God has sent His only begotten Son into the world **so that** [**ina**] we might live through Him.* *Oti's* B (= God sent Jesus into the world so that we might live through Him) <u>identifies</u> a specific manifestation of God's love <u>in</u> us and "<u>this</u>" (both are in *oti's* A). "We might live through Him" (*ina's* B) is clearly a desired outcome of *ina's* source A (God sending Jesus into the world): *ina's* A → B.

1John 5:13: *These things I have written to you who believe in the name of the Son of God, ᵇ**so that** [**ina**] you may know **that** [oti] you have eternal life.* *Oti's* B (you have eternal life) <u>identifies specifically</u> *oti's* A (what you may know) out of all that you may know. Knowing that you have eternal life (*ina's* B) is an available outcome of both key parts of *ina's* A: believing in the name of Jesus and John's writing to you believers. *Ina's* A → B and *oti* B's identifying A fit again in 5:13.

This list of John's *ina-oti* Scriptures on p. 65-68 has 18 *ina's* and 17 *oti's* in 15 contexts. Apx. 3 quotes <u>all</u> of John's *ina-oti* 1-verse-units plus 3 marked 2-verse-units (52 *ina's* and 53 *oti's* in 45 contexts). <u>My</u> <u>conclusion from all 45 contexts</u> is that <u>John clearly did not use *ina* as if</u> <u>it were *oti*</u>. John's use of both *ina* and *oti* in the same context illustrates what I have seen of John's consistency in 600+ uses of *ina* and *oti*.

KJV's Translation of John's Ina's As a Step in Forming a Perfect Storm

The KJV is an outstanding translation of Greek texts into English. The KJV's faithfulness to what the KJV translators judged to be the best texts (known then) makes it very trustworthy in many ways and gives it natural Scriptural authority for English-thinking believers. In this section we consider how the KJV translated John's *ina's*, so that we can see how simply this helped to form a "perfect storm" around *ina's* translation by outstanding trustworthy translators for centuries.

On p. 17-20 we discussed *ina*'s normally "telic" meaning: in *ina*'s usual form A *ina* B, source A might somehow lead to, cause, set up, precede, produce, result in, or extend to what B shows (*ina*'s A → B). The Greek word *telos* in the Bible projects to an "<u>end</u>" with <u>its</u> <u>extent</u>, <u>outcome</u>, <u>fulfillment</u>, or <u>purpose</u>. (Many use "telic" to refer only to purpose, but we can see that "purpose" does not fit John's *ina* and does exclude a Biblical meaning of *telos* found in Matt. 26:58, Rom. 6:21-22, 2Cor. 11:15, Heb. 6:11, James 5:11, and 1Peter 1:9). English words that express a telic *ina* include <u>so that</u>, <u>in order that</u>, in order to, with the result that, and for the purpose of. The simpler "that" is also telic <u>in some contexts</u> <u>but not others</u>: "that" has <u>many non-telic uses in English</u> and does <u>not by itself</u> <u>suggest</u> a telic meaning.

Chapter 7 shows *oti*'s 2 meanings: *oti* B may identify its A (<u>no arrow</u>) or show why A (<u>A ← B: *oti* = because</u>). Both differ from <u>*ina*</u> (<u>A → B</u>).

The KJV translates its 214 *ina*'s in John's Scriptures as follows:

* 166 are "that", which <u>is non-telic</u> by itself, but also <u>can be a shortened telic</u> (A → B, so that, in order that, ...);
* 35 are "to", normally a telic word <u>EXCEPT</u> in an <u>infinitive</u> (a 2-word-unit "to-verb") – <u>ALL 35 to's in the KJV are infinitives</u>;
* 8 translations are <u>clearly telic</u> (<u>projecting to</u> an end or <u>outcome</u>: 1 "to the intent", 1 "so that", and 6 "lest B = so that ... would not ...");
* the other 5 are not clearly telic (4 "for-to-verb" and 1 "so as").

The KJV is <u>truly ambiguous</u> in <u>translating *ina* and *oti* as "that"</u>: it comes from <u>166 *ina*'s</u> with its predominant <u>source A → outcome B telic</u> meaning and from 177 *oti*'s. In my judgment of each *oti*'s meaning shown on p. 116-117, this is <u>167 *oti* B's that identify A</u> plus 7 judged as "because" and 3 with both meanings. I also count about 10 that's as conjunctions from other Greek words.

In the KJV, what does "that" tell you when you see it? *Ina* or *oti* is a good indicator whether a statement is source-outcome or B may be identifying A, but the KJV "that" gives no guidance. If you see a KJV "that" and the context does not clearly show a source or outcome (as in a SIV, p. 59), is A a source and B its outcome (*ina*'s A → B)? Or does B identify A (no arrow or source-outcome relationship)? The Greek has predominant answers, but the KJV does not show them.

As stated, "to" usually projects toward an end (telic), but an infinitive itself is a 2-word-unit that is not telic. On p. 55-56 I illustrate this loss of the telic *ina* in John 4:34: *"My meat is to do the will of Him who sent Me..."* (KJV). "To do" is normally read as a 2-word-unit – a noun with its object that identifies "my meat" – instead of "to" projecting to an outcome: doing God's will. V. 34 shows how "to-verb" is ambiguous: it does not even suggest a telic meaning unless the context suggests it.

The KJV translates *ina* as the ambiguous "that" or "to" 201 of 214 times. The KJV's "that" for both 166 *ina* and 167 *oti* statements often give no hint of an A-B relationship even if it is a vital part of a verse's content (SIV's). The infinitive can likewise remove this content. For example, Jesus' prayer in John 17 has 19 *ina*'s, and the KJV translates 18 as "that" and 17:4 as the infinitive "to do". Chapter 4 shows major content lost for centuries with "that" for 6 of those *ina*'s.

This loss of content from the Greek is clear, but far greater losses are a key theme of John's Gospel, a likely foundation of 1-2John's initial receivers, a key message to them and for us, and authoritative sources of vital outcomes (this hinders moving into them). In Chapters 1-6 we saw 25 *ina*'s in which this relationship is a huge part of the content of a verse, and we found that *ina*'s usual telic meaning shows a vital picture that few believers have seen or considered there.

The superb KJV translators knew well the usual meaning of *ina* and these two basic meanings of *oti*. But they also found about 30 *ina*'s in John where the source A or its relationship to *ina*'s outcome B was hard to see: a true dilemma! The 400-year track record of English thinkers with John's *ina*-SIV's (Chapters 1-6) shows that we needed more guidance in these verses from KJV's outstanding translators that almost everywhere give us good reasons to trust them.

These great translators' usual excellence merely helps them do their part in previously producing and currently extending the "perfect storm" with *ina*. The KJV's great integrity amplifies any poor judgment in it. Their translating both *ina* and *oti* into English as the ambiguous "that" often loses Greek source-outcome content, and *ina* as "to-verb" can do likewise. As a result, for centuries probably most translators have not considered or even seen the telic-*ina*-theme in John's books for us.

Surveying 4 Major Translations of John's Ina's

Consider each version's translation below of the A – B relationship (*ina*'s telic A → B [so that…] vs. an ambiguous that, to…).

213 *ina*'s in Updated NAS: 92 so that; 53 that; 54 to; 14 miscellaneous.

213 *ina*'s in ESV: 50 so that (includes 5 "lest" [telic by its meaning] and 1 "in order that"); 83 that; 64 to; 16 miscellaneous.

25 *ina*-SIV's in the KJV: 24 that, 1 to (John 4:34)

25 *ina*-SIV's in the Updated NAS: 23 that, 2 to (John 4:34, 1John 3:8)

25 *ina*-SIV's in the ESV: 19 that, 2 to (John 4:34, 1John 3:8), 1 no word (13:34b), 1 colon (1John 4:21), 2 so that (John 15:17, 2John 6b)

25 *ina*-SIV's in the RSV: 22 that, 3 to (John 4:34, 15:17, 1John 3:8)

How the New Insights Fit Into the True Gospel and New Testament

What is the practical change by a purely telic *ina* by John? It does not change what we need to be doing (obey all that He tells us and His commandments, love one another, believe in Jesus, manifest His nature…). But believers have suffered a systematic loss of SOURCES of vital desired outcomes caused by not translating *ina* as purely telic. A purely telic *ina* greatly changes how we can move long-term into

God's calling for us: we <u>first connect</u> to our loving Father through the Lord Jesus, and <u>then stay connected in the loving fellowship</u> with Him and one another that John 15 and 1John describe. <u>This will produce all of the things</u> that we should be <u>doing with Him</u>. Staying in this life-giving fellowship includes Jesus' sacrifice to justly restore this if any of us disrupts it by a sin. A telic *ina* in 22 verses consistently provides a clear revelation of "abide in Jesus" as a <u>true theme</u> of John and 1John.

If anyone finds only 5 or 10 clear exceptions – as Chapter 8 shows, I find 0 out of 213 – then we could call *ina* "predominantly telic". IF anyone concludes John's *ina* is predominantly telic, then believers can check how those few exceptions affect the existence and authority of this unveiled theme in John's Gospel and Epistles. I personally expect that finding 10 real exceptions is extraordinarily unlikely, and that any number of real exceptions will not touch the existence of John's theme.

{ Here I parenthetically mention a few other themes of John's Gospel, so that readers know explicitly that I do not claim this unveiled theme in John to be its central theme, but merely a very important and rarely seen theme. Of greatest importance is revealing Jesus' unique relationship to His Father, and with this is the Holy Spirit's relationship to Both. Second is God's great love manifested by Jesus for everyone in the world, and especially as a personal Father for all who become His children through Jesus. Other key themes include this unveiled theme of our staying in this special fellowship and life in Jesus, our loving one another, our believing into Jesus, and more. Again, I insert this paragraph to show a balance that I do not seek for this book. }

Chapter 7 completes the foundation for *ina* in this book. Chapter 8 and Apx. 1-3 are encyclopedic in nature: arranged in an order where you can find and read what you want. For some readers, Chapter 8 as a unit or for selected *ina*-verses could be a major part of this book (like Chapter 7 is), while any section in an appendix is more elective.

Chapter 8

Each of John's *Ina*'s Can Be Telic

I quote every *ina* in John's writings from the Updated New American Standard Bible with <u>its translation</u> of **ina boldfaced**. I also show how each *ina* can be telic. My <u>criterion for telic</u> is <u>a projected end, outcome, or extent B</u> of a <u>source or start A</u> (A → B). In the usual form A *ina* B, I identify A, B, antecedents, a relevant "this", a fuller discussion of a verse on another page, or anything else if I believe it will help probable users of Chapter 8. I may not comment if a telic meaning seems obvious to me. If the Updated NAS translates *ina* as a telic like "so that", then I consider this as one indicator (more is needed) that this verse is unlikely to disrupt John's purely telic *ina* and might not need explaining. If I judge that a context makes the *ina* clearly telic even with translations like the ambiguous "that" or "to" (both can be telic but often are not telic), then I may not comment.

* means "quoted in another place", either with extra explanation or with other related verses. The small number at the end is the reference page(s), as illustrated by the "ₚ. 19" in *John 1:7-8 below.

** means I think a reference adds <u>significant</u> explanation or context to that provided in this Chapter 8, as illustrated by "ₚ. 99, 100" in **John 1:27.

* John 1:7-8: *⁷He came as a witness, **to** testify about the Light, **so that** all might believe through him. ⁸He was not the Light, but he came **to** testify about the Light.* John came as a witness (source A), and a witness <u>may</u> <u>testify</u> (<u>outcome B</u>). Both "to-verb's" are literally <u>so that he could</u> testify...: every *ina*-subjunctive–verb translated as "to" could be expanded like this, but often in Chapter 8 I shall not. All 3 *ina* B's in v. 7-8 clearly are <u>outcomes</u> of each source A. A → B ₚ. 19

John 1:19: *...when the Jews sent to him [John] priests and Levites from Jerusalem **to** ask him, "Who are you?"* source A → outcome B

* John 1:22: *...Who are you, **so that** we may give an answer to those who sent us?...* The question A should lead to outcome B: A → B _{p. 19}

** John 1:27: *It is He who comes after me, the thong of whose sandal I am not worthy **to** untie.* "Not worthy to untie" shows how unworthy John is compared to Jesus: <u>a telic-extent</u> with an exceptional format (not A *ina* B), and it is best to see all about both on p. <u>99-101</u>. _{p. 99, 100}

** John 1:31: *I did not recognize Him, but **so that** He might be manifested to Israel, I came baptizing in water.* B is written first (showing its priority) instead of its usual place after A *ina*: I came baptizing in water so that He might be... (A *ina* B). You see that v. 31's <u>*ina* B A format did not disturb *ina*'s telic relationship</u> (source A → outcome B). _{p. 99-100}

* John 2:25: *...because He did not need anyone **to** testify concerning man, for He Himself knew what was in man.* Jesus did not need anyone to be a source of producing this outcome: testifying concerning man. The telic source A → outcome B. _{p. 128}

John 3:14-15: *... must the Son of Man be lifted up;* [15]***so that** whoever believes will in Him have eternal life.* Telic: source A → outcome B

John 3:16: *For God so loved the world, that He gave His only begotten Son, **that** whoever believes in Him shall not perish, but have eternal life.* The context makes B (v. 16 after *ina*) a clear outcome with "that".

John 3:17: *For God did not send the Son into the world **to** judge the world, but **that** the world might be saved through Him.* Two *ina*'s: both are literally, *in order that* [*He would judge...* and *the world could be...*]. *Ina*'s telic meaning (source A → outcome B) is clear in v. 17 even with the often non-telic "that" and "to" for each *ina*. (Like 12:47 on p. 81).

John 3:20: *For everyone who does evil hates the Light, and does not come to the Light **for fear that** his deeds will be exposed.* "His deeds getting exposed" is telic *ina*'s <u>projected outcome</u> of coming to the Light, and therefore he fears and avoids coming to it (Him). "...<u>so that</u> his deeds <u>would not</u> be exposed": many translations say well, "<u>lest</u> his deeds be exposed". "Lest" also fits John 12:35, 12:40, 12:42, 18:28, 2John 8, Rev. 9:4, 9:5, 9:20, 11:6, 13:17, 16:15, 18:4, and still others.

* John 3:21: *But he who practices the truth comes to the Light, **so that** his deeds may be manifested as having been wrought in God.* V. 21 after *ina* is a projected outcome of coming to the Light (A): A → B. _{p. 65}

John 4:8: *For His disciples had gone away into the city **to** buy food.* Clearly telic (source A → outcome B) even with "to".

John 4:15: *...Sir, give me this water, **so** I will not be thirsty nor come all the way here to draw.* so = so that. Source A sets up outcome B.

** John 4:34: *Jesus said to them, "My food is* **to** *do the will of Him who sent Me and* **to** *accomplish His work."* One *ina* is translated at 2 places in order to provide clarity in English. P. 12-14 explain how a telic *ina* works well in v. 34 (a SIV: Spiritually Informative Verse). ₚ. ₁₂-₁₄

John 4:36: *Already he who reaps is receiving wages and is gathering fruit for life eternal;* ᵇ**so that** *he who sows and he who reaps may rejoice together.* V. 36 after *ina* is an outcome of its source, v. 35-36a.

John 4:47: *When he heard that Jesus had come out of Judea into Galilee, he went to Him and was imploring Him* **to** *come down and heal his son; for he was at the point of death.* Imploring Jesus was the source A for outcome B: He comes down and heals the father's son.

John 5:7: *The sick man answered Him, "Sir, I have no man* **to** *put me into the pool when the water is stirred up, but while I am coming, another steps down before me."* The sick man looked for this desired outcome B: getting help into the water at the right time – I have no man (source A) so that I might get this outcome. source A → outcome B

John 5:14: *...Behold, you have become well; do not sin anymore,* **so that** *nothing worse happens to you.* 5:14 fits into the "lest" list in 3:20.

John 5:20: *For the Father loves the Son, and shows Him all things that He Himself is doing; and the Father will show Him greater works than these,* **so that** ᵇ*you will marvel.* B (v. 20b) comes out of A (v. 19-20a).

John 5:22-23: *...He has given all judgment to the Son,* ²³**so that** *all will honor the Son even as they honor the Father. He who does not honor the Son does not honor the Father who sent Him.* Father God gave all judgment to the Son (source A) in order to produce this outcome B: all would honor Him as they honor the Father. A → B

John 5:34: *But the testimony which I receive is not from man, but* ᵃ*I say these things* **so that** ᵇ*you may be saved.* Ina's B (34b) does not identify these things Jesus said (A), but is A's desired outcome (like John 8:6).

* John 5:36: *But the testimony which I have is greater than the testimony of John; for* ᵃ*the works which the Father has given Me* **to** ᵇ*accomplish – the very works that I do – testify about Me, that the Father has sent Me.* Father God gave Jesus works to do (source A) with this intended outcome B: He would accomplish (fulfill) them. Jesus did them, and they provided a testimony that the Father did send Jesus. ₚ. ₆₅

John 5:40: *and you are unwilling to come to Me* **so that** *you may have life.* Again, B (have life) is an outcome of A: coming to Jesus (6:37-40).

* John 6:5: *Therefore Jesus...said to Philip, "Where are we to buy bread,* **so that** *these may eat?"* "People eating" (B) is the projected

outcome of buying bread (A). "People eating" and "buying bread" are different actions. Again, the telic source A → outcome B p. 65

John 6:7: *Philip answered Him, "Two hundred denarii worth of bread is not sufficient for them, **for** everyone **to** receive a little."* 200 denarii worth of bread was the insufficient source A for providing this desired outcome B: everyone would receive a little bread (literally, …for them so that each could receive a little). A → B

John 6:12: *…Gather up the leftover fragments **so that** nothing will be lost.* Gathering the fragments (source A) had this projected outcome: nothing would be lost (outcome B).

John 6:15: *So Jesus, perceiving that they were intending to come and take Him by force **to** make Him king, withdrew again to the mountain by Himself alone.* They intended to come and seize Jesus (A) for this purpose or desired outcome: <u>so that they would</u> make Him their king.

** John 6:28-30: *[28]Therefore they said to Him, "What shall we do, **so that** we may work the works of God?" [29]Jesus answered and said to them, "<u>This is the work of God, **that** you believe</u> in Him whom He has sent." [30]So they said to Him, "What then do You do for a sign, **so that** we may see, and believe You? What work do You perform?"* The projected outcome of the *ina*'s in v. 28 and 30 are clear and translated well. V. 29 is a "<u>this</u> is A *ina* B" with a poorly seen "this" (a SIV), and is usually translated as if the *ina* were *oti*. We explicitly discuss the underline in v. 29 as a feature on p. 14-17. There we see that <u>the telic ina</u> works extremely well in v. 29, <u>John 6</u>, and <u>John 4-6</u>. p. 14-17

John 6:37-40: *[37]<u>All that the Father gives Me will come to Me</u>, [b]and the one who comes to Me I will certainly not cast out. [38]For I have come down from heaven, [b]not **to** do My own will, but the will of Him who sent Me. [39a]<u>This</u> is the <u>will of Him who sent Me</u>, [b]**that** of all that He has given Me <u>I lose nothing, but raise it up</u> on the last day. [40a]For <u>this</u> is the <u>will of My Father</u>, [b]**that** everyone who beholds the Son and believes in Him will have eternal life, and I Myself will raise him up on the last day.*

In v. 38, Jesus came from heaven was a source A for its outcome B: doing <u>His Father's will</u> over His own will. His coming from heaven (A) <u>preceded</u> and set up what He did and not do on earth (B). For *ina* in v. 39, the <u>antecedent for "This" in v. 39 is v. 37-38</u>, especially <u>all that the Father gives Jesus comes to Him</u> (v. 37a). God's will that all of them come to Jesus ("This" and "God's will" in v. 39a) is this *ina*'s source leading to v. 39b's outcome: Jesus loses nothing but raises each one up on the last day. V. 40a looks like v. 39a, but in v. 40 "this" and "My Father's will" refer to losing nothing in v. 39b. This last *ina*'s outcome is again Jesus raising each one up on the last day in v. 40b, plus its added truth and outcome of eternal life.

John 6:50: *This is the bread which comes down out of heaven, **so that** one may eat of it and not die.* Jesus identified Himself in John 6:48 as "the bread from heaven", = "This". "Eat of it [this bread] and not die" (*ina*'s B) is not identifying the bread or "This", but is an outcome produced by this bread coming down out of heaven (source A).

John 7:3: *...Leave here and go into Judea, **so that** Your disciples also may see Your works which You are doing.* Jesus' brothers commanded Him (source A) for a projected outcome B: His disciples see His works.

** John 7:23: *If a man receives circumcision on the Sabbath **so that** the Law of Moses will not be broken, are you angry with Me because I made an entire man well on the Sabbath?* Circumcision on the Sabbath (source A) was intended to produce this outcome B: not breaking the Law of Moses, as the NAS translates well. ₚ. ₆₅

John 7:32: *...the chief priests and the Pharisees sent officers **to** seize Him.* Seizing Jesus was the desired outcome of or purpose for the leaders' sending officers (A), and seizing Jesus does not identify A or anything in it: source A is before outcome B in order to produce it.

John 8:6: *They were saying this, testing Him, **so that** ᵇthey might have grounds for accusing Him...* 8:6b is the purpose (desired outcome B) for what they said as they tested Him (source A). Outcome B clearly does not identify what they said: the "this" in v. 6 is identified in v. 4-5.

John 8:56: *Your father Abraham rejoiced **to** see My day, and he saw it and was glad.* Even as Abraham anticipated God's raising Isaac from the dead if that was needed to fulfill His word (Heb. 11:19), Abraham saw Jesus' day by faith and rejoiced as he anticipated this outcome or telic end result: God's work to fulfill a humanly impossible need. What is Jesus' day? One answer is God's work 2000 years ago to redeem hopelessly-fallen mankind. Abraham could see this work by faith, rejoice in God, and thereby continue with Him until seeing this telic end from heaven. Another possible Jesus' day he could see was Jesus' coming bodily in Gen. 18 to set up fulfilling God's promise of Isaac.

John 8:59: *Therefore they picked up stones **to** throw at Him, but Jesus hid Himself and went out of the temple.* They picked up stones (A) in order to throw them at Him (B). B is an intended outcome of source A.

John 9:2-3: *And His disciples asked Him, "Rabbi, who sinned, this man or his parents, **that** he would be born blind?" ³Jesus answered, "It was neither that this man sinned, nor his parents; but it was **so that** the works of God might be displayed in him."* In v. 2 the disciples asked who sinned (source A) to cause this man to be born blind (a projected outcome B of sin). Jesus answer in v. 3 shows neither one's sin caused his blindness (first *ina*'s <u>outcome B</u>), but "the works of God displayed in him" (2nd *ina*'s B) would be <u>a greater outcome</u> of his blindness.

** John 9:22: *His parents said this because they were afraid of the Jews; for the Jews had already agreed **that** if anyone confessed Him to be Christ, he was to be put out of the synagogue.* Logically the B in v. 22 could either identify what was agreed or be the intended outcome from the agreement (5:34, 8:6, and 11:41-42 are clearly outcomes and not identifying). A telic *ina* in 9:22 shows John's insight that <u>their agreeing</u> (source A) was <u>intended to produce this outcome</u> B: to <u>intimidate</u> any person out of confessing Christ and to punish anyone who did. _{p. 65-66}

John 9:36: *He answered, "Who is He, Lord, **that** I may believe in Him?"* B is an outcome of learning A. As always for John's *ina*, A → B.

John 9:39: *And Jesus said, "For judgment I came into this world, **so that** those who do not see may see, and that those who see may become blind."* B (all after *ina*) clearly is a projected outcome of source A (His coming into this world).

John 10:10: *The thief comes only **to** steal and kill and destroy; I came **that** they may have life, and have it abundantly.* The content of v. 10 is translated well. Both telic-*ina*'s emphasize that the two statements are <u>contrasting</u> <u>intended outcomes</u> of the thief and Jesus coming. A → B

John 10:17: *For this reason the Father loves Me, because I lay down My life **so that** I may take it again.* "I lay down My life" is source A.

John 10:31: *The Jews picked up stones again **to** stone Him.* Like John 8:59, this context makes an infinitive (to stone) clearly telic.

** John 10:38: *but if I do them, though you do not believe Me, believe the works, **so that** you may know and understand that the Father is in Me, and I in the Father.* Again, the telic source A → outcome B _{p. 51-52, 130}

John 11:4: *But when Jesus heard this, He said, "This sickness is not to end in death, but for the glory of God, **so that** the Son of God <u>may be glorified</u> by it."* Jesus' being glorified (B) is <u>an outcome</u> of A: <u>God's glory</u> as He caused the sickness that <u>killed Lazarus</u> to <u>not end in death</u>. {I <u>underline the subjunctive-B-verbs</u> in John 11-17 (p. 78-86, 141-146).}

John 11:11: *This He said, and after that He said to them, "Our friend Lazarus has fallen asleep; but I go, **so that** I <u>may awaken</u> him out of sleep."* Jesus tells His disciples, I go (source A) for this purpose or projected outcome B: to wake Lazarus up.

John 11:15: *and I am glad for your sakes that I was not there, **so that** you <u>may believe</u>; but let us go to him.* "I was not there" (before Lazarus died) was a source A to set up outcome B: the disciples would believe.

John 11:16: *Therefore Thomas…said to his fellow disciples, "Let us also go, **so that** we __may die__ with Him."* Going with Jesus (source A) would lead to this __projected outcome B__: dying with Him.

John 11:19: *and many of the Jews had come to Martha and Mary, __to console__ them concerning their brother.* Like 11:31.

John 11:31: *Then the Jews who were with her in the house, and consoling her, when they saw that Mary got up quickly and went out, they followed her, supposing that she was going to the tomb __to weep__ there.* V. 19 and 31 are clearly telic source-outcome A → B by content.

John 11:37: *But some of them said, "Could not this man, who opened the eyes of the blind man, have kept this man also **from** __dying__?"* NAS translates the content very well, but literally it is, "__make so that__ this man would not have died". This says Jesus could have made (source) this __outcome__: "Lazarus not dying". Again, *ina* is a clearly telic A → B.

John 11:41-42: [41]*…Then Jesus raised His eyes, and said, "Father, I thank You that You have heard Me.* [42]*I knew that You always hear Me; but because of the people standing around I said it, **so that** [b]they __may believe__ that You sent Me."* The content and context are clear: __Jesus said__ "Father, I thank You that You have heard Me" (A) with a __projected outcome__ stated after *ina*: "they may believe that You sent Me" (v. 42b). "It" after "said" is __not in Greek__, but every translator I checked added this or it, confirming to readers that __v. 42b__ does __not__ __identify what He said__. (Like 5:34 and 8:6, *ina* B in 11:42 does not identify A, but is A → B).

John 11:50-52: [50]*nor do you take into account that it is expedient for you **that** [b]one man __die__ for the people, and that the whole nation not __perish__…*[52]*and not for the nation only, [b]but **in order that** He __might__ also __gather__ together into one the children of God who are scattered abroad.* In v. 50, __expedient for you__ A led to __outcome__ B: one man dying for the people with the whole nation not perishing. V. 50b-52a form the __new source A__ for v. 52's *ina*, and its outcome B is "Jesus may also gather into one the children of God scattered abroad" (v. 52b). Both A → B.

John 11:53: *So from that day on they planned together **to** __kill__ Him.* V. 53 is like 12:10 and 9:22 (or 11:57) with its source-outcome note.

John 11:55: *Now the Passover of the Jews was near, and many went up to Jerusalem out of the country before the Passover **to** __purify__ themselves.* A clearly telic source A → outcome B even with "to".

John 11:57: *Now the chief priests and the Pharisees had given orders **that** if anyone knew where He was, he was __to report__ it, so that they* *might seize Him.* As in John 9:22, the B after *ina* logically could be the outcome the orders were intended to produce or could identify what they were. A telic *ina* tells us that B was an <u>intended outcome</u> of the orders (source A): these leaders were acting with stealthy intentions.

John 12:7: *Therefore Jesus said, "Let her alone,* **so that** *she <u>may keep</u> it for the day of My burial."* Many translations say, "she had kept it": both times are possible because the aorist subjunctive does not imply a time of action. Letting her alone (source A) set up this outcome (B): she could anoint Jesus for His burial then and maybe also later.

John 12:9: *The large crowd of the Jews then learned that He was there; and they came, not for Jesus' sake only, but* **that** *they <u>might</u> also <u>see</u> Lazarus, whom He raised from the dead.* Many came (source A) in order to see Lazarus (projected outcome B of their coming) in addition to seeing Jesus.

John 12:10: *But the chief priests planned* **to** <u>**put**</u> *Lazarus* <u>to death</u> *also.* Notice again 11:53 and the note on John 9:22.

John 12:20: *Now there were some Greeks among those who were going up* **to** <u>worship</u> *at the feast.* As normal, a source A → outcome B

John 12:23: *And Jesus answered them, saying, "The hour has come* **for** *the Son of Man* **to** <u>be glorified</u>*."* The time had come (<u>source A</u>) for Jesus to be glorified (B): the key <u>outcome</u> to be produced then. A → B

John 12:35: *...Walk while you have the Light,* **so that** *darkness <u>will</u> **not** <u>overtake</u> you; he who walks in the darkness does not know where he goes.* Walking while having the Light is source A to <u>prevent</u> outcome B.

John 12:36: *While you have the Light, believe in the Light,* **so that** *you <u>may become</u> sons of Light...* The NAS clearly shows this telic *ina*.

John 12:37-38: *...yet they were not believing in Him.* [38]*This was* **to** <u>fulfill</u> *the word of Isaiah the prophet which he spoke: "Lord, who has believed our report? And to whom has the arm of the Lord been revealed?"* "This" in v. 38 was their not believing in Jesus in v. 37: both form the A in "A *ina* B". The literal *ina* B outcome starts with "so that the word of Isaiah the prophet which he spoke would be fulfilled". This is the first of 9 *ina*-verses in John's Gospel with "'to fulfill' a word or Scripture" (John 13:18, 15:25, 17:12, and 5 in John 18-19): in general, a <u>source A sets up its outcome B</u> of fulfilling that "word or Scripture".

John 12:40: *He has blinded their eyes and He hardened their heart,* **so that** *they <u>would</u> **not** <u>see</u> with their eyes and <u>perceive</u> with their heart, and <u>be converted</u> and I heal them.* Everything after "so that" is an outcome B from the source A: blinded eyes and a hardened heart.

John 12:42: *Nevertheless many even of the rulers believed in Him, but because of the Pharisees they were not confessing Him,* **for fear that** *they* <u>would be put out</u> *of the synagogue.* They did not confess Jesus (source A) <u>so that</u> they <u>would not</u> be put out of the synagogue, in order to prevent that projected outcome B. (Like John 3:20, p. 74). A → B

John 12:46: *I have come as Light into the world,* **so that** *everyone who believes in Me* <u>will</u> *not* <u>remain</u> *in darkness.* The telic ina is clear (but the future indicative translation comes from a Greek subjunctive-B-verb).

John 12:47: *If anyone hears My sayings and does not keep them, I do not judge him; for I did not come* **to** <u>judge</u> *the world, but* **to** <u>save</u> *the world.* Nearly identical to John 3:17 (p. 74), but here both ina's are translated "to", and the source A → outcome B is clear with all 4 ina's.

John 13:1: *Now before the Feast of the Passover, Jesus knowing that His hour had come* **that** *He* <u>would depart</u> *out of this world to the Father...* Again (like John 12:23), B is an outcome of His hour coming.

John 13:2: *During supper, the devil having already put into the heart of Judas Iscariot, the son of Simon,* **to** <u>betray</u> *Him.* Betraying Jesus was the devil's intended outcome B of what he had put into Judas' heart (source A).

John 13:15: *For I gave you an example* **that** *you also* <u>should do</u> *as I did to you.* Jesus <u>gave His disciples His example</u> (A) in order to <u>produce outcome</u> (B): <u>they do</u> as He did to them. V. 1-14 identify His example.

John 13:18: *I do not speak of all of you. I know the ones I have chosen;* ^b*but it is* **that** *the Scripture* <u>may be fulfilled,</u> *"He who eats My bread has lifted up his heel against Me."* Here A is <u>not</u> <u>written</u>, but is <u>easy to</u> <u>know</u>. From John 12:4-6 and 13:2, 10-11, 21-30, and v. 18a, <u>A</u> is <u>the</u> <u>disciple Judas being among them</u>: he was not truly following Jesus and for a while was intending to betray Him (John 12:4, 13:2, and 13:27). <u>Judas' being among them</u> (source A) produced its <u>outcome</u> B: <u>fulfilling</u> <u>the Scripture quoted in v. 18</u> (He who eats My bread...). The need to identify an <u>unwritten (implied) A</u> in v. 18 with a clearly valid solution in a very large context can be an example to help us realize that a true A might not be easy to identify or not be clearly stated, as with the ina's in 1-2John that are often thought to act like *oti*. p. 102-103 identifies possible hard-

to-see A's, and 17:12 (p. 85) identifies 13:18's A (Judas) more explicitly

John 13:19: *From now on I am telling you before it comes to pass,* **so that** *when it does occur, you* <u>may believe</u> *that I am He.* A → B p. 131, 14:29

John 13:29: *For some were supposing, because Judas had the money box, that Jesus was saying to him, "Buy the things we have need of for the feast"; or else,* **that** *he* <u>should give</u> *something to the poor.*

Disciples supposed that Jesus was <u>saying</u> a statement to Judas <u>to produce this outcome</u>: giving to the poor. <u>IF</u> *ina* were used <u>as if</u> it were *oti* in v. 29, then v. 29 would show that Jesus told Judas, "Give something to...". But the Bible never shows Jesus telling a disciple, "give something" or "just do something", but He said the specific thing to be given or done. <u>Therefore some would not suppose</u> Jesus said, "You should give <u>something</u>": a telic *ina* <u>fits v. 29 better</u>.

** John 13:34: *A new commandment I give to you,* **that** *you <u>love</u> one another, even as I have loved you,* **that** *you also <u>love</u> one another.* V. 34 is explained as a main feature on p. 21-23, with more on p. 46 and insight into v. 34's key "large context of John 15" on p. 24-27. _{p. 21-23, 46}

John 14:3: *If I go and prepare a place for you, I will come again and receive you to Myself,* ^b**that** *where I am, there you <u>may be</u> also.* V. 3a (source A) leads to this projected outcome B: the disciples will be where Jesus is (v. 3b). As normal, *ina*'s telic source A → outcome B.

John 14:13: *Whatever you ask in My name, that will I do,* **so that** *the Father <u>may be glorified</u> in the Son.* source A → outcome B

John 14:16: *I will ask the Father, and He will give you another Helper,* **that** *He <u>may be</u> with you forever.* "He may be with you forever" is an outcome B of source A (I...another Helper). This outcome B contrasts with the disciples' situation with Jesus at the time of statement A.

John 14:29: *Now I have told you before it happens,* **so that** *when it happens, you <u>may believe</u>.* V. 29 is like 13:19, and clearly telic like it.

** John 14:31: *but* **so that** *the world <u>may know</u> that I love the Father, I do exactly as the Father commanded Me. Get up, let us go from here.* The unusual *ina* B A: the intended outcome (dependent clause) was written before the source statement. Doing exactly as the Father commanded Jesus (source A) produced an outcome B: letting the world know that He loves the Father. Again, the slightly altered format (not A *ina* B) does <u>not</u> change *ina*'s A → B. _{p. 66, 100 rewrite 14:31 as A *ina* B}

 * John 15:2: *Every branch in Me that does not bear fruit, He takes away; and every branch that bears fruit,* ^b*He prunes it* **so that** *it <u>may bear</u> more fruit.* V. 2b's source-outcome telic *ina* is clear (A is He prunes it). P. 24-27 show how each *ina* in 15:1-17 can easily be telic. _{p. 24-27}

** John 15:7-8: *If you abide in Me, and My words abide in you, ask whatever you wish, and it will be done for you.* ⁸*My Father is glorified by this,* **that** *you <u>bear</u> much fruit, and so prove to be My disciples.* "This" in v. 8 refers to the asking and receiving while abiding (v. 7): this glorifies God and produces an outcome B of bearing much fruit, which will prove our being Jesus' disciples. In contrast, *oti* in v. 8 or "that" in translations would show "English-thinking believers" that bearing much fruit is glorifying Father God: "that" or a non-telic *ina* in v. 8 veils the insight in v. 7-8 that "asking and receiving in our abiding life in Jesus" is glorifying God and a SOURCE of v. 8's outcome (bearing fruit). p. 8-9

* John 15:11: *These things I have spoken to you **so that** My joy may be in you, and that your joy may be made full.* The telic *ina* in John 15:1-17 is featured in p. 24-27, but v. 11's telic *ina* seems evident. Also, v. 11's second "that" comes from v. 11's only *ina*. p. 9, 24-25

** John 15:12: *This is My commandment, **that** you love one another, just as I have loved you.* Featured on p. 22-27. p. 22-27

** John 15:13: *Greater love has no one than this, **that** one lay down his life for his friends.* Often included with v. 12 on p. 22-27. p. 22-27

** John 15:16-17: *You did not choose Me but I chose you, and appointed you **that** you would go and bear fruit, and that your fruit would remain, **so that** whatever you ask of the Father in My name He may give to you. [17]This I command you, **that** you love one another.* A telic *ina* in John 15:17 and in all of v. 1-17 is the feature of p. 24-27. p. 24-27

* John 15:24-25: *If I had not done among them the works which no one else did, they would not have sin; but now they have both seen and hated Me and My Father as well. [25]But they have done this **to fulfill** the word that is written in their Law, "They hated Me without a cause."* "They have done this" is not in the Greek, but is inserted by the translator to represent their hating Jesus and God shown in v. 24. V. 25 is useful for this whole book, because v. 25 shows an "*ina* B" with an "easily-identified but easy-to-miss in the Greek" A, the source of B. V. 24 (their hating Jesus and His Father) is *ina*'s source A for its outcome B: to fulfill the quoted Scripture (literally, in order that the word may be fulfilled...). A $\rightarrow$ B p. 103

John 16:1: *These things I have spoken to you **so that** you may be kept from stumbling.* *Ina*'s telic source A $\rightarrow$ outcome B

John 16:2: *They will make you outcasts from the synagogue, but an hour is coming **for** everyone who kills you **to think** that he is offering service to God.* B describes a very self-deceiving outcome of a source A (making "you" outcasts...). John 12:23, 13:1, and 16:32 have "*ina*-B outcomes" of a source, "an hour coming" (another part of A in v. 2). p. 80

** John 16:4: *But these things I have spoken to you, **so that** when their hour comes, you may remember that I told you of them. These things I did not say to you at the beginning, because I was with you.* The NAS shows all 3 key translations: a **telic *ina*** and the two underlined *oti's* with *oti's* two basic meanings. p. 66 explains v. 4 if the NAS's v. 4 is not clear to you

John 16:7: *But I tell you the truth, it is to your advantage* **that** *I go away*... Giving "advantage to the disciples" was a source or cause A for the outcome B (Jesus' going away) that came soon after Jesus said this. *Ina*'s telic source A → outcome B

John 16:24: *Until now you have asked for nothing in My name; ask and you will receive,* **so that** *your joy may be made full.* A → B like 15:7-11

John 16:30: *Now we know that You know all things, and have no need* **for** *anyone* **to question** *You; by this we believe that You came from God.* Literally, You...have no need (A) so that one should "question" (*erōtaō*) You. As we saw (p. 47), *erōtaō* asks more presumptively than *aiteō*: here Jesus' disciples realize He did not need them to question Him (outcome B) like speakers normally need to speak the full truth.

* John 16:32: *Behold, an hour is coming, and has already come,* **for** *you* **to be scattered,** *each to his own home, and* to leave *Me alone; and yet I am not alone, because the Father is with Me.* The time had come (source A) for this soon-to-be-produced event or outcome B: each disciple would be scattered and would leave Jesus alone. p. 66, 80 (12:23)

John 16:33: *These things I have spoken to you,* **so that** *in Me you may have peace. In the world you have tribulation, but take courage; I have overcome the world.* As normal, the telic source-outcome A → B

Note: Jesus' prayer in John 17 provide a concentration of 19 *ina*'s (9% of John's total uses) and combine to show *ina*'s emphasis on desired or projected outcomes instead of already accomplished facts.

John 17:1: *Jesus spoke these things; and lifting up His eyes to heaven, He said, "Father, the hour has come; glorify Your Son,* **that** *the Son may glorify You."* The Father glorifying Jesus (source A) set up or led to this outcome B: Jesus glorifying the Father – showing His presence and key features of His true nature better than ever.

John 17:2: *even as You gave Him authority over all flesh,* **that** *to all whom You have given Him, He may give eternal life.* Giving eternal life is a desired outcome B from Father God giving Jesus authority over all flesh (source A). As with all of John's *ina*'s, I conclude a telic A → B

** John 17:3: *This is eternal life,* **that** *they may know You, the only true God, and Jesus Christ whom You have sent.* A telic *ina* in v. 3 reveals that eternal life is a source of a key desired outcome B: we come to know (*ginōskō*) Father God and Jesus – get to know God relationally and experientially (p. 29-30). In contrast, "that B" in v. 3 is normally read as if *ina* were *oti* and would identify a key feature of eternal life – not a key outcome that we should be using this source to develop. P. 29-30 add to this discussion. P. 103 explains "This" that starts v. 3. _{p. 29-30, 103}

John 17:4: *I glorified You on the earth, having accomplished the work which You have given Me **to do**.* Literally, ... work You have given Me so that I would do: Jesus was given the work to do <u>before</u> He did it (B).

** John 17:11: *I am no longer in the world; and yet they themselves are in the world, and I come to You. Holy Father, KEEP them in Your name, the name which You have given Me, **that** they <u>may be</u> one even as We are.* <u>Father God keeping Jesus' disciples in Their name</u> leads to the special unity that is like God's oneness and like Jesus prayed for us in 17:21: the 11 <u>becoming one</u> <u>was</u> <u>an OUTCOME</u> (B) <u>OF HIS KEEPING</u> (source A), <u>not</u> <u>a work to do</u> <u>to cause</u> or <u>identify</u> His keeping. A → B _{p.30}

John 17:12: *While I was with them, I was keeping them in Your name which You have given Me; and I guarded them and not one of them perished but the son of perdition, **so that** the Scripture <u>would be fulfilled</u>.* The son of perdition perishing is the source A for its *ina* B.

John 17:13: *But now I come to You; and these things I speak in the world **so that** they <u>may have</u> My joy made full in themselves.* "They" after *ina* are the 11 disciples (v. 11-12), which makes clear the telic *ina* and the <u>connection of 17:13 with John 15:11</u>. A → B

John 17:15: *I do not ask You **to take** them out of the world, but **to keep** them from the evil one.* <u>Verbs like ask, agree, desire, and, command</u> are often followed by *ina* to show the <u>intended goal or outcome</u> of what was asked, agreed, desired.... If *oti* followed any of these verbs, this would normally identify the specific request.... Often a verb action and its intent are the same, but if *oti* and *ina* keep their distinct meanings, then an *oti* or a telic *ina* could add an insight or prevent a misleading impression (as in John 8:6, 9:22, or 11:57, but irrelevant in 17:15, 24). In v. 15, both *ina*'s are "ask–*ina*–subjunctive-verb in B" and translated as "to": this has good features of being simple, concise, and not veiling a big difference in a telic vs. a non-telic meaning.

John 17:19: *For their sakes I sanctify Myself, **that** they themselves also <u>may be</u> sanctified in truth.* As usual, a telic source A → outcome B

** John 17:20-21: *I do not ask on behalf of these alone, but for those also who believe in Me through their word; [21]**that** they <u>may</u> all <u>be</u> one; even as You, Father, are in Me and I in You, **that** they also <u>may be</u> in Us, **so that** the world <u>may believe</u> that You sent Me.* Jesus' asking for us who believe through their word (v. 20) should lead to this outcome: we become one like God is one and like the 11 disciples were to become one (17:11). This A and B are the next *ina*'s A for its B (be <u>in God like 15:4-10</u>), which sets up the third *ina*'s B (the world's belief). _{p. 30-31, 66-67}

** John 17:22-23: *The glory which You have given Me I have given to them,* **that** *they* <u>*may be*</u> *one, just as We are one;* [23]*I in them and You in Me,* **that** *they* <u>*may be*</u> *perfected in unity,* **so that** *the world* <u>*may know*</u> *that You sent Me, and loved them, even as You have loved Me.* Jesus has given us believers His glory from His Father (source A) to lead us to the first *ina*'s outcome B: to be one like He and His Father, with Both in us (John 14:20, 15:4). This glory lets God with His nature manifest in our lives. His continued work in us and manifesting out of us (15:4-17, 17:22) lead to 17:23's first *ina*'s outcome: we believers will be <u>perfected in unity</u>. In turn, "our being perfected in unity" is a key source A of "the world coming to know that Father God sent Jesus and loves us like Him" (B). P. 30-32 feature a discussion of v. 20-23: I conclude a telic source A → outcome B for all 6 *ina*'s in v. 20-23. _{p. 30-32}

** John 17:24: *Father, I desire* **that** *they also, whom You have given Me,* <u>*be*</u> *with Me where I am,* **so that** *they* <u>*may see*</u> *My glory which You have given Me, for You loved Me before the foundation of the world.* "Desire *ina*" is discussed with John 17:15 on p. 67 and 85. The second *ina* is translated well and discussed with insights on p. <u>67</u>. A → B _{p. 67}

** John 17:26: *and I have made Your name known to them, and will make it known,* **so that** *the love with which You loved Me* <u>*may be*</u> *in them, and I in them.* NAS's telic is clear ("<u>name = nature</u>" adds insight: <u>p. 32</u>). Here I stop underlining subjunctive-B-verbs in John 11-17. _{p. 32}

* John 18:8-9: *Jesus answered, "I told you that I am He; so if you seek Me, let these go their way,* [9]*to fulfill the word which He spoke, 'Of those whom You have given Me I lost not one.'"* "Let these go" (A) is a source of outcome B: fulfilling Jesus' word of losing none. The context makes *ina*'s <u>telic</u> meaning clear, so that "to" is fine <u>in this verse</u>. _{p. 67}

John 18:28: *Then they led Jesus from Caiaphas into the Praetorium, and it was early; and they themselves did not enter into the Praetorium* **so that** *they would* **not** *be defiled, but might eat the Passover.* A → B

John 18:31-32: *...The Jews said to him* [Pilate], *"We are not permitted to put anyone to death,"* [32]**to** *fulfill the word of Jesus which He spoke, signifying by what kind of death He was about to die.* The Jews not being permitted to put anyone to death (A) is a source of this <u>outcome</u>: fulfilling Jesus' spoken word about His death (B).

John 18:36: *Jesus answered, "My kingdom is not of this world. If My kingdom were of this world, then My servants would be fighting* **so that** *I would not be handed over to the Jews; but as it is, My kingdom is not of this realm."* Jesus' servants would fight (source A) to cause this projected outcome B: He would not be handed over to the Jews.

John 18:37: *Therefore Pilate said to Him, "So You are a king?" Jesus answered, "You say correctly that I am a king. For* <u>this</u> *I have been born, and for* <u>this</u> *I have come into the world,* **to** *testify to the truth. Everyone who is of the truth hears My voice."* "'To testify'" is again a good short way to say, "in order that I may testify". A telic *ina* in v. 37 shows that "<u>Jesus' birth and coming into the world destined to be a king</u>" is v. 37's "this", and both are the <u>source A</u> of producing this <u>outcome B</u>: <u>with authority He could testify to the truth</u>.

John 18:39: *But you have a custom* **that** *I release someone for you at the Passover; do you wish then that I release for you the King of the Jews?* The custom is a source A of this projected outcome B: Pilate would release someone for the Jews at Passover.

John 19:4: *Pilate came out again and said to them, "Behold, I am bringing Him out to you* **so that** *you may know that I find no guilt in Him."* As with each of John's *ina's*, I conclude source A → outcome B.

John 19:16: *So he then handed Him over to them* **to** *be crucified.* A telic source A → outcome B is again clear even with "to".

John 19:24: *So they said to one another, "Let us not tear it, but cast lots for it, to decide whose it shall be"; this was* **to** *fulfill the Scripture: "They divided My outer garments among them, and for My clothing they cast lots."* Their agreeing to cast lots for Jesus' tunic (source A) led to this outcome B: fulfilling the quoted Scripture.

John 19:28: *After this, Jesus, knowing that all things had already been accomplished,* **to** *fulfill the Scripture, said, "I am thirsty."* This is not "A *ina* B": I re-write v. 28 in the A *ina* B format on p. 100. Source A – "Jesus said, 'I am thirsty'" – set up outcome B: fulfilling the Scripture (A → B). ("Knowing that all things were already accomplished" is an appositive that brings out an insight about Jesus at that moment but does not affect this telic *ina*.) _{p. 100}

John 19:31: *Then the Jews, because it was the day of preparation,* **so that** *the bodies would not remain on the cross on the Sabbath (for that Sabbath was a high day),* <u>asked</u> *Pilate* **that** *their legs* <u>might</u> *be broken, and that they* <u>might</u> *be taken away.* Being the day of preparation is the first *ina's* source A that caused the Jews' to desire outcome B: bodies would not remain on the cross on the Sabbath. The "asked Pilate *ina*" is discussed with John 19:38 when that identical phrase occurs again.

* John 19:35: *And he who has seen has testified, and his testimony is true; and he knows that he is telling the truth,* **so that** *you also may believe.* As with all of John's *ina's*, a telic source A → outcome B. _{p. 58}

John 19:36: *For these things came to pass* **to** *fulfill the Scripture, "Not* *a bone of Him shall be broken."* "These things" (in A) are especially 19:31-34. Their outcome is *ina* B: fulfilling Scriptures in v. 36-37.

John 19:38: *After these things Joseph of Arimathea, being a disciple of Jesus, but a secret one for fear of the Jews,* <u>asked</u> *Pilate* **that** *he might take away the body of Jesus; and Pilate granted permission. So he came and took away His body.* "After these things" refers to the things identified in John 19:1-34. A <u>telic *ina*</u> shows the <u>desired outcome of the asking</u> instead of what they asked Pilate. The difference is little in v. 38 but clear in v. 31. In v. 31, the Jews did <u>not say to Pilate</u> that the legs <u>might</u> be broken (B), <u>but asked him</u> <u>to get the outcome</u> of legs broken and their bodies taken away. With a telic *ina* in v. 38, Joseph asked Pilate to get <u>this outcome B</u>: Joseph would take away Jesus' body.

** John 20:31: *but these have been written* **so that** *you may believe that Jesus is the Christ, the Son of God; and* **that** *believing you may have life in His name.* John's writing (source A) had a <u>desired outcome</u> "so that you may believe that Jesus is the Christ..." (B), with <u>its further outcome</u> (2nd *ina*'s B): having life in Jesus' name. Source A for the final *ina* is all of v. 31 up to the second *ina*. Both *ina*'s are A → B. p. 131

Chapters 5-6 better show the context of all 1John *ina*-verses and further explain all **. The first 5 *ina*'s in 1John 1-2 are easily-seen telic.

** 1John 1:3-4: ^{3}*what* <u>we</u> *have seen and heard we* <u>proclaim to you also</u>, **so that** <u>you too</u> <u>may have fellowship with us</u>; *and indeed* <u>our fellowship is with the Father, and with His Son Jesus Christ</u>. *These things we write,* **so that** *our joy may be made complete.* p. 35, 41

* 1John 1:9: *If we confess our sins, He is faithful and righteous* **to** *forgive us our sins and to cleanse us from all unrighteousness.* "...so that He would forgive..." shows more truth than "...to forgive...": His forgiving and cleansing us are an <u>outcome</u> of <u>His</u> faithful and just <u>nature</u>. p. 43-44

* 1John 2:1: *My little children, I am writing these things to you* **so that** *you may not sin. And if anyone sins, we have an Advocate with the Father, Jesus Christ the righteous.* A → B p. 43-44

* 1John 2:19: *They went out from us, but they were not really of us; for if they had been of us, they would have remained with us; but they went out,* **so that** *it would be shown that they all are not of us.* p. 41, 44, 67

** 1John 2:27a: *As for you, the anointing which you received from Him abides in you, and you have no need for anyone* **to** *teach you;* As in John 16:30 (p. 84), this literally is "you have no need (source A) <u>so that</u> one should teach you (outcome B)." For more about the content, p. 41-42 quote most of 2:19-29 and p. <u>44</u> clarifies this "no need". p. 42, 44

** 1John 2:28: *Now, little children, <u>abide in Him,</u>* **so that** *when He appears, we may have confidence and not shrink away from Him in shame at His coming.* *Ina* in v. 28 is clearly telic, but v. 28 has another feature: we can see much evidence that the underlined command to abide in Him is <u>the command</u> in all 1John that initial 1John receivers <u>had already known well</u>. I call this "the 1John commandment" (Chapter 5 shows its key to 1John, and especially to 1John 3-5). p. 36-37, 42

** 1John 3:1: *<u>See how great a love</u> the Father has bestowed on us,* **that** *we would be called children of God; and such we are. For this reason the world does not know us, because it did not know Him.* The Father's great love bestowed on us (A) <u>leads to this outcome B</u>: we are called His children – clearly telic and true! Consider a bigger A: 2:28-3:1a. <u>What is a special way</u> to see God's great love? Only two verses before 3:1, 1John 2:28 commands us to abide (stay) in Christ – a short way to <u>identify the fellowship</u> in <u>1:1-4, all 1John, and John 15</u>. <u>This abiding fellowship in Christ</u> helps us <u>see and experience</u> God's great love.

This <u>great love to us</u> <u>extends so far</u> that we may be called God's children (*ina's* B), and John affirms we are. 1John 3:1 is 1 of John's 5 likely telic-extents. As we see for John 15:13 on p. 25, 26, and 100-101, this "possible telic-extent" merely adds another telic meaning to a verse that already has a reasonable "telic-outcome". p. 44, 100-101, 104, 110

** 1John 3:5: *You know that <u>He appeared</u>* **in order to** *take away sins; and in Him there is no sin.* As the NAS shows clearly, Jesus appeared is *ina's* source A and taking away sins is *ina's* outcome B. V. 8 adds another outcome of His appearing, and v. 5-8 are tightly connected. My quote and explanation of v. 5-8 are on p. 45 and here I simply show the telic *ina* in v. 5 and in 3:8 below. A → B p. 45, 68

** 1John 3:8: *the one who practices sin is of the devil; for the devil has sinned from the beginning. The <u>Son of God appeared</u> for this purpose,* *^bto destroy the works of the devil.* *Ina* in v. 8 shows that destroying the works of the devil is an outcome B of Jesus' appearing (in source A). Taking away sins in 3:5 is another outcome of His appearing: He came in order to <u>break us loose from sin</u>, which destroys a basic work of the devil in mankind from our beginning. V. 5-8 are quoted and explained on p. <u>45</u>, which I highly recommend for v. 5-8. Here I simply state that v. 5-8a (or v. 4-8a) before v. 8's *ina* is its antecedent-source A and identifies "this purpose" in v. 8. p. 45 (p. 104 provides the same discussion as p. 45)

** 1John 3:11: *^aFor <u>this is the message</u> which <u>you have heard</u> <u>from the beginning,</u> ^bthat we should love one another.* V. 11's telic *ina* is easy to see after realizing v. 11's "the beginning": it is near the beginning of each believer's life-giving fellowship that all of 1John describes (p. <u>40</u>).

As v. 11 shows, initial 1John readers heard a message THEN that should lead to this outcome B: we love one another. What is v. 11's "message heard from the beginning"? To abide (stay) in Jesus, a short way to say: "stay in this special fellowship in Him" that 1John describes and 1John 2:28 repeats (p. 35-42). So 1John 3:11 concisely REMINDS believers to stay in this fellowship with God and His true children: abide in Him is source A for outcome B in v. 11b, love one another. p. 40-42, 45

** 1John 3:23: *This is His commandment, **that** we believe in the name of His Son Jesus Christ, and love one another, just as He commanded us.* God's command (singular) is to abide in Him (stay in this life-giving fellowship). It will produce v. 23's 2 outcomes: we believe in the name of His Son Jesus Christ and love one another. John did not miscount 1 instead of 2, or add the second command as an afterthought. To avoid taking v. 23 out of its true 1John context, I recommend the explanation about 3:22-24 on p. 37-38 or 35-42. p. 35-42, especially p. 37-38

1John 4:9: *By this the love of God was manifested in us, that God has sent His only begotten Son into the world **so that** we might live through Him.* "Ina B" (= so that we might live through Him) clearly is a desired outcome of source A (= God sending Jesus into the world).

** 1John 4:16-17: *...[b]God is love, and the one who abides in love abides in God, and God abides in him. [17]By this, love is perfected with us, **so that** we may have confidence in the day of judgment; because as He is, so also are we in this world.* "Ina = so that" is translated well. "This" in v. 17a refers to the abiding fellowship in v. 16b, in v. 12-16 four times, or in all of 1John (the inclusive 1John commandment in 1John 2:28 fits well again in 4:21 and in 5:3). 4:12, 13, 15, and 16 are quoted on p. 38-39, and 4:12-17 is discussed as a unit on p. 46. p. 38-39, 46, 106

** 1John 4:20-5:1: *[20]...one who does not love his brother...cannot love God...[21]And this commandment we have from Him, **that** [b]the one who loves God should love his brother also. [1]Whoever believes that Jesus is the Christ is born of God, and whoever loves the Father loves the child born of Him.* As explained on p. 38-39 and 106, 4:12-21 has no command; assuming a command in 4:21b does not fit its context in 4:20 and 5:1; and 1John's singular command to abide in Him fits well with a telic ina in 4:21 and no command in 4:12-21. 1John's command is to stay in the loving fellowship with Father God, His Son Jesus, and His other children (1John 1:1-4, 4:12-16): staying in it is the source A of this ina's outcome B, to love both one's brother and God. p. 38-39, 106

** 1John 5:2b-3: *[2]...when we love God and observe His commandments. [3]For this is the love of God, **that** we keep His commandments; and His commandments are not burdensome.* God's love (in ina's A) is a great source of outcome B: we keep His commandments. *"We love, because He first loved us"* (1 John 4:19, 5 verses back); *"If you love Me, you will keep My commandments"* (John 14:15 in many texts); and *"If anyone loves Me, he will keep My word"* (John 14:23). "His commandments are not burdensome" also comes from His love. 1John 5:3 can help us realize Jesus' terms in John 15:9-10: "stay in My love" includes "keep My commandments" (p. 46-47).

A good antecedent for "this" as 5:3 begins might <u>not be obvious to us</u>, but can be identified. All of 1John and <u>this specific section of it</u> (<u>4:7-5:3</u>) emphasize the <u>loving, life-giving fellowship</u> with God and His children, and initial 1John receivers are treated like they know it well. It provides two excellent meanings of "this": this fellowship, and 5:2's "<u>love God</u> and <u>observe</u> [*poieō, do*] His commandments" that are key features of this fellowship. Either meaning of "this" is <u>a part of the love of God</u> (A) that empowers us to keep all His commands. _{p. 46-47, 106-107}

* 1Jn 5:13: *These things I have written to you who believe in the name of the Son of God, **so that** you may know that you have eternal life.* Knowing that we have eternal life (*ina's* B) is a desired outcome of *ina's* A: both believing in the name of Jesus and John's writing to them. The NAS shows this A-B source-outcome well. A → B ₚ. 42, 68

** 1John 5:16: ᵃ*If anyone sees his brother committing a sin not leading to death, he shall ask and God will for him give life to those who commit sin not leading to death.* ᵇ*There is a sin leading to death; I do not <u>say that</u> he should make request for this.* John did not say v. 14-16a to cause this outcome: <u>requesting presumptively</u> (a <u>bad outcome</u> of 16a) for those who commit a sin leading to death. John is <u>still emphasizing</u> "ask God according to His will" (v. 14-16a use a humbler word for "ask" 4 times: p. <u>47</u>). "*Ina* as if *oti*" in v. 16 would indicate that "make request for this" identifies what John did not say: he did not say many things, so "*ina* as if *oti*" obscures the instruction (to <u>ask according to His will</u> in v. 14-16a) that a telic *ina* in v. 16b brings out. ₚ. 47

1John 5:20: *And we <u>know</u> that the Son of God has come, and has given us understanding **so that** we may <u>know</u> Him who is true; and we are in Him who is true, in His Son Jesus Christ. This is the true God and eternal life.* The telic *ina* is clear. See p. 137 for "know" in v. 20.

** 2John 5-6: *Now I ask you, lady, not as though I were writing to you a new <u>commandment</u>, but <u>the one</u> which we have had <u>from the beginning</u>, **that** we love one another.* ⁶*And <u>this</u> is <u>love</u>, **that** we walk according to His commandments. This is <u>the commandment</u>, just as you have heard <u>from the beginning</u>, **that** you should walk in it.*

V. 5-6 show much evidence that the lady (v. 5) had the same good "beginning of each one's life in Jesus" as the initial receivers of 1John (p. 47-48, 42): the first A *ina* B is like the 1John 3:11 "reminder" (p. 89-90: "<u>abide in Jesus</u>" is a command, message [precept], <u>and</u> word). The second A *ina* B is like 1John 5:3 (p. 90, and quoted directly across the page from 2John 6: the tiny differences are [God's] love, and "keep vs. walk according to" His commands). Like v. 5's A *ina* B, the third *ina*'s source A is a singular command (like 1John 2:7-8, 3:23 and 4:21), and its outcome B (to walk in it) is consistent with the 1John outcomes (as explained on p. 35-42 and <u>47-49</u>). Both telic *ina*'s and the singular command heard from the beginning in v. 5 and v. 6 help us to realize that John gave <u>brief reminders</u> in both books. _{p. 35-42, 47-49, 90, 91}

2John 8: *Watch yourselves,* **that** *you do* **not** *lose what we have accomplished, but* <u>*that*</u> *you may receive a full reward.* Clearly, both receiving a full reward and not losing what "we" accomplished (B) are intended outcomes of watching ourselves (source A). The underlined "<u>that</u>" is not in the Greek, but rightly comes from the first *ina*.

2John 12: *Though I have many things to write to you, I do not want to do so with paper and ink; but I hope to come to you and speak face to face,* **so that** *your joy may be made full.* source A → outcome B

** 3John 4: *I have no greater joy than* <u>*this*</u>, **to** *hear of my children walking in the truth.* P. 100-101 quote 3John 2-4 and show all 5 of John's telic-extents: we can see that each <u>identifies how great</u> a thing (God's love twice, signs, how unworthy, <u>things that bring joy</u>) can "<u>figuratively</u> go" or extend. A telic-extent can identify a term in A because the extent (telic) is figurative and is not a sequential outcome. In 3John 4, *toutōn* is the genitive plural "of these things" – not the underlined "this". These things can refer to v. 2's prosperity, health, Gaius' soul prospering, brethren <u>testify of his truth</u> (v. 3), and <u>his actual walking in truth</u> (v. 3's end). Of these things in v. 2-3, <u>his walking in the truth</u> goes farther (A → B) in a <u>figurative</u> direction (joy). V. 4 says: "of these things, to hear of my children <u>walking</u> in the truth" (v. 3's end) brings the <u>greatest joy</u>. _{p. 100-101}

3John 8: *Therefore we ought to support such men,* **so that** *we may be fellow workers with the truth.* As with all of John's *ina*'s, a telic A → B.

Rev. 2:10: *Do not fear what you are about to suffer. Behold, the devil is about to cast some of you into prison,* **so that** *you will be tested, and you will have tribulation for ten days. Be faithful until death, and I will give you the crown of life.* The telic source-outcome is clear. I add that my Greek sources show the subjunctive B-verb, or "could be tested".

Rev. 2:21: *I gave her time* <u>**to repent**</u>, *and she does not want* <u>*to repent*</u> *of her immorality.* With *ina*'s source-outcome, Jesus' giving her time was the source A of the desired outcome B: she would repent. "Time" differs from "repent": clearly *ina* B does not identify A like *oti* B. You also see that each "to repent" reads as a unit without a telic meaning: both look alike, but the second "to repent" is a non-telic Greek infinitive and the first in Greek is *"I gave her time ina [so that] she could repent"* – a clearly telic A → B that illustrates again John's *ina-oti* difference.

Rev. 3:9: *Behold, I will cause those of the synagogue of Satan, who say that they are Jews and are not, but lie – I will make them [ina] come and bow down at your feet, and make them know that I have loved you. Ina* is not translated in v. 9: the A *ina* B part of v. 9 says, *"I will make them* [source A] **so that** *they shall come and shall bow down at your feet and shall know that I have loved you"* (B is after "so that"). You can see B as a projected outcome of source A (telic *ina*'s A → B).

Rev. 3:11: *I am coming quickly; hold fast what you have,* **so that** *no one will take your crown.* Clearly source A (hold fast) → outcome B.

Rev. 3:18: *I advise you to buy from Me gold refined by fire* **so that** *you may become rich, and white garments* **so that** *you may clothe yourself, and that the shame of your nakedness will not be revealed; and eye salve to anoint your eyes* **so that** *you may see.* The "so that's" make this verse's telic source A → outcome B clear for all 3 *ina*'s. Here I merely add that the NAS inserted the underlined "that" (not in Greek) as a shortened form of the previous "so that".

Rev. 6:2: *I looked, and behold, a white horse, and he who sat on it had a bow; and a crown was given to him, and he went out conquering and* **to** *conquer.* Conquering was what he did and his intended outcome B of his going out A. Notice that projecting into the intended future is the only addition of "*ina* conquer" (subjunctive) to "conquering".

Rev. 6:4: *And another, a red horse, went out; and to him who sat on it, it was granted to take peace from the earth, and* **that** *men would slay one another; and a great sword was given to him.* "Men would slay one another" is the outcome B of the source A: the one sitting on the red horse was granted permission to take peace from the earth.

Rev. 6:11: *And there was given to each of them a white robe; and they were told* **that** *they should rest for a little while longer, until the number of their fellow servants and their brethren who were to be killed even as they had been, would be completed also.* A telic *ina* in v. 11 shows "the outcome of what they were told" but not necessarily what they were told (unlike John 5:34…, this distinction has little effect in Revelation).

Rev. 7:1: *After this I saw four angels standing at the four corners of the earth, holding back the four winds of the earth,* **so that** *no wind would* *blow on the earth or on the sea or on any tree.* source A → outcome B

Rev. 8:3: *Another angel came and stood at the altar, holding a golden censer; and much incense was given to him, **so that** he might add it to the prayers of all the saints on the golden altar which was before the throne.* "Adding the incense to prayers" (B) in no way identifies being given incense, but is an outcome of his being given incense (source A).

Rev. 8:6: *And the seven angels who had the seven trumpets prepared themselves **to** sound them.* Ina's consistent source A → outcome B

Rev. 8:12: *The fourth angel sounded, and a third of the sun and a third of the moon and a third of the stars were struck, **so that** a third of them would be darkened and the day would not shine for a third of it, and the night in the same way.* Striking these things is the source A for desired outcome B: to darken them. 7:1, 8:6, 9:15, 12:4… are likewise.

Rev. 9:4: *They were told **not to** hurt the grass of the earth, nor any green thing, nor any tree, but only the men who do not have the seal of God on their foreheads.* With a telic *ina*, whatever was told them (source A) authorized this outcome B: they could not hurt vegetation, but only the unsealed people.

Rev. 9:5: *And they were **not** permitted **to** kill anyone, but **to** torment for five months; and their torment was like the torment of a scorpion when it stings a man.* The 2 B's show stated outcomes of their permission A.

Rev. 9:15: *And the four angels, who had been prepared for the hour and day and month and year, were released, **so that** they would kill a third of mankind.* source A (release 4 angels) → outcome B (killing)

Rev. 9:20: *The rest of mankind, who were not killed by these plagues, did not repent of the works of their hands, **so as not to** worship demons, and the idols of gold and of silver and of brass and of stone and of wood, which can neither see nor hear nor walk.* This unusual translation of *ina* easily shows source A (not repenting) leading to its projected outcome B: the rest of mankind continued in their evil, foolish worship of demons and idolatry. Telic *ina's* source A → outcome B.

Rev. 11:6: *These have the power to shut up the sky, **so that** rain will **not** fall during the days of their prophesying; and they have power over the waters to turn them into blood, and to strike the earth with every plague, as often as they desire.* Clearly a telic source A → outcome B.

Rev. 12:4: *And his tail swept away a third of the stars of heaven and threw them to the earth. And the dragon stood before the woman who was about to give birth, **so that** when she gave birth he might devour her child.*

Rev. 12:6: *Then the woman fled into the wilderness where she had a place prepared by God, **so that** there she would be nourished for one thousand two hundred and sixty days.*

Rev. 12:14: *But the two wings of the great eagle were given to the woman, **so that** she could fly into the wilderness to her place, where she was nourished for a time and times and half a time, from the presence of the serpent.*

Rev. 12:15: *And the serpent poured water like a river out of his mouth after the woman, **so that** he might cause her to be swept away with the flood.* All *ina*'s in Rev. 12 are clearly telic source A → outcome B.

** Rev. 13:12-13: *He exercises all the authority of the first beast in his presence. And he makes the earth and those who dwell in it **to** worship the first beast, whose fatal wound was healed. [13]He performs great signs, **so that** he even makes fire come down out of heaven to the earth in the presence of men.* In v. 12 "he makes" this outcome B: worship of the first beast. In v. 13, *ina* B is not strictly A's outcome, but shows how great the signs (A) can be. So *ina* retains its telic property here of showing how far A can figuratively go or extend.   p. 19; p. 101 explains

Rev. 13:15: *And it was given to him to give breath to the image of the beast, **so that** the image of the beast **would** even speak and **cause** as many as do not worship the image of the beast **to** be killed.* V. 15's first *ina* is clearly telic and is clearly translated that way (A → B). For the second *ina* (which many Greek texts omit), "would make so that...would be killed" is translated well as "(would) cause...to be killed": this shows a source producing an outcome with or without *ina*.

Rev. 13:16-17: *And he causes all, the small and the great, and the rich and the poor, and the free men and the slaves, **to** be given a mark on their right hand or on their forehead, [17]and he provides **that** no one will be able to buy or to sell, except the one who has the mark, either the name of the beast or the number of his name.* "He provides" at the beginning of v. 17 is not in the Greek: v. 17 starts with, "and so that no one could buy or sell except..." In Greek, v. 17 is "and *ina* outcome" and shows more of what the second beast would make, do, or cause (*poieō* is in each verse from v. 12 to early in v. 16 – 8 times). Therefore we see that v. 17 really is a telic *ina* B with *ina*'s A spread out over v. 12-16, and the NAS probably inserted "he provides" because *ina*'s real antecedent A is so large and spread out.   P. 107 shows v. 12-17 quoted together

Rev. 14:13: *And I heard a voice from heaven, saying, "Write, 'Blessed are the dead who die in the Lord from now on!'" "Yes," says the Spirit, "**so that** they may rest from their labors, for their deeds follow with them."* B (after *ina* = so that) is clearly an outcome, but what is A? I believe "the blessing with the Spirit's affirmation of it (the ongoing present tense Yes)" is a good "source A" of the outcome B (they may rest from their labors), so that this *ina* is also telic.

Rev. 16:12: *The sixth angel poured out his bowl on the great river, the Euphrates; and its water was dried up, **so that** the way would be prepared for the kings from the east.* A → B

Rev. 16:15: *("Behold, I am coming like a thief. Blessed is the one who stays awake and keeps his clothes, **so that** he will **not** walk about naked and men will not see his shame.")* source A → outcome B

Rev. 18:4: *I heard another voice from heaven, saying, "Come out of her, my people, **so that** you will **not** participate in her sins and [ ] receive of her plagues."* Two "*ina* not's", but the first "so that" carries over well to the not "receive of her plagues" (the NAS shows the source-A-[*ina*-not]-outcome-B in English for both *ina*'s).

Rev. 19:8: *It was given to her **to** clothe herself in fine linen, bright and clean; for the fine linen is the righteous acts of the saints.* The subject of "was given" can refer to "the bride making herself ready" (v. 7b). A telic *ina* in v. 8 shows she was given what she needed so that she would clothe herself in bright and clean fine linen. If John used *ina* like *oti*, then "clothing herself" could identify what she was given (fine linen). Therefore whether this "clothing herself" is an outcome of or else what she was given is decided by whether John's *ina* can act like *oti*. It was given to her because she would clothe herself in bright and clean fine linen is a third possible meaning if *ina* could act like *oti* in Rev. 19:8.

Rev. 19:15: [15]*From His mouth comes a sharp sword, **so that** with it He may strike down the nations, and He will rule them with a rod of iron; and He treads the wine press of the fierce wrath of God, the Almighty.*

Rev. 19:17-18: [17]*...Come, assemble for the great supper of God,* [18]***so that** you may eat the flesh of kings and the flesh of commanders and the flesh of mighty men and the flesh of horses and of those who sit on them and the flesh of all men, both free men and slaves, and small and great.* In both 19:15 and 18, the telic source A → outcome B is clear.

Rev. 20:3: *and he threw him into the abyss, and shut it and sealed it over him, **so that** he would not deceive the nations any longer, until the thousand years were completed; after these things he must be released for a short time.* V. 2's binding Satan and v. 3 before *ina* are the source A of his not deceiving the nations any longer (outcome B).

Rev. 21:15: *The one who spoke with me had a gold measuring rod **to** measure the city, and its gates and its wall.* The speaker having a rod (source A) led to *ina*'s outcome B: he would use it to measure the city, its gates, and its wall.

Rev. 21:23: *And the city has no need of the sun or of the moon **to** shine on it, for the glory of God has illumined it, and its lamp is the Lamb.* In the outcome B, God's glory replaces a need for the sun or moon to shine (source A). As in John 2:25, 16:30, and 1John 2:27, this "need A" is an implied normal need – not written explicitly as a need in this Biblical context.

Rev. 22:14: *Blessed are those who wash their robes, **so that** they may have the right to the tree of life, and may enter by the gates into the city.*   In Rev. 22:14 as we found with each of John's *ina*'s:

source (or start) A → projected outcome (or extent) B

Index of John's *Ina*-Verses Outside of Chapter 8 with *Ina* Discussed

John		John	
1:7, 1:22	p. 19	19:4	p. 134
1:27, 1:31	p. 99, 100	19:28	p. 100, 134
2:25	p. 128	19:35	p. 58, 135
3:21	p. 65, 128	20:31	p. 135
4:34	p. 12-14, 55-56, 59, 70, 111		
5:36	p. 65, 128	1John	
6:5	p. 65, 129	1:3-4	p. 35
6:15	p. 129	1:9, 2:1	p. [8], 43-44
6:28-30	p. 14-17	2:19	p. 67-68, 135
6:29	p. 14-17, 59	2:27	p. 42, 44
6:38	p. 129	3:1	p. 44, 101, 104, 110, 135
7:3	p. 109	3:5	p. 45, 68, 104, 135
7:23	p. 65, 129	3:8	p. 45, 56, 104, 136
9:22	p. 65-66, 129-130	3:11	p. 40, 45, 48, 67, 105, 136
10:17	p. 130	3:23	p. 37-38, 59, 105, 136
10:38	p. 52, 130	4:9	p. 68, 105, 137
11:15	p. 67, 100, 130	4:17	p. 46, 67, 105-106, 137
11:31	p. 130	4:21	p. 38-39, 59, 106
11:41-42	p. 130-131, 140	5:3	p. 46-47, 48, 106-107, 111
11:50	p. 131	5:13	p. 68, 137
12:9	p. 131	5:16	p. 47, 140
13:1	p. 131	5:20	p. 137
13:18	p. 102-103		
13:19	p. 131	2John 5-7	p. 47-49, 59, 67, 138
13:29	p. 131-132, 140	3John 4	p. 101
13:34, 15:12-17	p. 21-23, 46, 59		
14:31	p. 66, 100, 132	Revelation	
15:1-17	p. [5-9], 21-23, 24-27	3:9	p. 112, 138
15:12-13	p. 25, 26, 100	3:11	p. 112
15:25	p. 103, 132	3:18	p. 138
16:4	p. 66, 132	6:4, 6:11	p. 112
16:30	p. 132-133	8:3	p. 112-113
16:32	p. 66, 133	9:4, 9:5, 9:20	p. 113
17:3	p. 29-30, 103	13:12	p. 113
17:11	p. 30, 32	13:13	p. 19, 101
17:20-23	p. 30-32, 66-67, 133	13:12-17	p. 107
17:24	p. 67, 133-134	14:13	p. 107, 113
17:26	p. 32	18:4	p. 113-114
18:9	p. 67, 134		
18:37	p. 134	[Matt. 5:29]	p. 17, 146

Appendix 1

Complete Groups of *Ina*-Verses

The basic purpose of Apx. 1-3 is to make it easier to check my analysis of *ina* by those who want to see how *ina* has a telic nature in <u>any</u> or <u>every</u> verse in John's writings. I seek to form useful complete groups of *ina*'s and *oti*'s so that a reader can see the actual evidence about this amazing discovery and will draw valid conclusions. Apx. 1 forms four complete groups of *ina*-verses in John's writings in order to show all exceptions to three properties of *ina*, and to facilitate useful contrasts with John's use of *oti*. (Apx. 2 shows more about John's *oti*, and Apx. 3 further compares how John used *ina* and *oti*).

Every Non- "A Ina B" Verse in John's Writings

I more clearly describe a telic meaning of *ina* in every verse of John's writings by using *ina*'s predominant form, A *ina* B, with A being the source or start and B being a projected (possible) telic-outcome or telic-extent. In this section of Apx. 1, I re-write all "other-forms" into A *ina* B, so that you can check for a loss of real content, a real change in the A-B relationship, or a violation of a purely telic *ina* in the Scripture or its re-write. I find <u>no noteworthy change in any verse</u>, so that I ignore mentioning "*ina* B A" except for these verses and this section.

John 1:27: *It is He who comes after me,* [b]*the thong of whose sandal I am not worthy to untie.* <u>Check for no loss of content or A-B relationship in re-writing</u> v. 27b, *"I am not worthy to untie the thong of whose [His] sandal."* The Greek word order is closer to the re-write than to a divided-B in "B_2 A *ina* B_1". <u>See</u> John 1:27 in the <u>next section</u>.

John 1:31: *... but so that He might be manifested to Israel, I came baptizing in water.* The subordinate clause is written first (because of its importance) instead of its usual place after A. You may check for no loss of real content or change in source A → outcome B in my re-write: *"I came baptizing in water* **so that** *He might be manifested to Israel."* The *ina* is clearly telic in the *ina* B A and in its A *ina* B re-write.

John 11:15a: *and I am glad for your sakes* <u>that</u> *I was not there* [A], **so that** *you* <u>may believe</u> [B].... The NAS wrote A *ina* B for this <u>Greek *ina* B A</u> (= ...***ina*** *you may believe* [*ina* outcome B], *oti I was not there* [*ina*'s source A]). { In v. 15 <u>*oti*</u> can <u>identify</u> what Jesus is glad about for them and <u>show why He is glad</u> (*oti*=because). In both Greek and the NAS, "<u>I was not there</u>" is <u>a source</u> of <u>both</u> <u>outcomes</u>: *ina* you may believe, and "<u>A-*oti*=because</u>" (= I am glad for your sakes because). With arrows as on p. 62 and a new A, B, C as in John 17:24 on p. 67, I write: A ← *oti* "source B" *ina* → C, or A ← source B → C (2 outcomes). }

John 14:31: *but* **so that** *the world may know that I love the Father, I do exactly as the Father commanded Me....* Check for no loss of content or change in A-B source-outcome: *"But I do exactly as the Father commanded Me* **so that** *the world may know that I love the Father."* _{p. 66}

John 19:28: *After this, Jesus, knowing that all things had already been accomplished,* **to** *fulfill the Scripture, said, "I am thirsty."* Check for no loss of content or change in A-B relationship in my re-write: *"After this, knowing that all things had already been accomplished, Jesus said, 'I am thirsty', so that the Scripture would be fulfilled."* _{p. 87}

Every Ina Telic-Extent Verse in John's Writings

John 1:27: *It is He who comes after me, the thong of whose sandal I am not worthy* **to** *untie.* Or consider v. 27b's re-write on p. 99: "I am not worthy **to** untie the thong of His [*whose*] sandal." In either form, "to untie" (= so that I may untie) <u>shows how unworthy</u> John is compared to Jesus: <u>a telic-extent</u> like 3John 4 and Rev. 13:13 (both on p. 101).

John 15:12b-13: ¹²...<u>you love one another, just as I have loved you</u>. ¹³*Greater love has no one than* <u>this</u>, ***that*** *(ina) one lay down his life for his friends.* The "this" in v. 13 can naturally be v. 12b: "as I have loved you" <u>matches v. 13b's content</u> of "laying down His life for His friends". A telic *ina* shows that one laying down his life for his friends (B) can be an <u>outcome</u> <u>and</u> <u>extent</u> of "this" and the "greater love has no one". As an <u>outcome</u>, v. 13 shows that Jesus' love for us is the greatest love and <u>can lead to His further layiing and our laying down our lives for our friends</u>. A <u>telic-extent</u> is <u>not needed for a telic-*ina* in v. 13</u>, but does <u>add a good insight</u>: the greatest love extends (<u>figuratively</u>) so far that one may lay down his life like He did. Notice that <u>a telic-extent</u> lets *ina*'s B identify "how great" and "this" in *ina*'s A with *ina* being telic.

1John 3:1: *See how great a love the Father has bestowed on us,* [b]***that*** *we would be called children of God; and such we are. For this reason the world does not know us, because it did not know Him.* The Father's great love bestowed on us (source A) leads to this outcome B: we are called His children – clearly telic and true! The larger source A, the 3 verses 2:28-3:1a, is quoted and discussed on p. 104, but here we discuss this telic-extent. This great love to us is so great (extends so far) that we could be called children of God (*ina*'s B), and John affirms we truly are. As we saw for John 15:13 (p. 100), this telic-extent adds a second telic meaning to a verse that has a very fitting "telic-outcome".

3John 2-4: [2]*Beloved, I pray that in all respects you may* prosper *and be in* good health, *just as* your soul prospers. [3]*For I was very glad when brethren came and* testified to your truth, [b]*that is, how* you are walking in truth. [4]*I have no greater joy than* this, [b]***to** hear of* my children walking in the truth. To see v. 4's telic, realize that *toutōn* is the plural genitive "of these things", not v. 4's underlined "this". These things can refer to v. 2's prosperity, health, Gaius' soul prospering, v. 3a's brethren testify to his truth, and his actual walking in it in v. 3b: all are desired features in our life in Jesus. Of these things, his walking in the truth goes farther in causing joy (telic: to or toward an end, a figurative A → B with A = v. 2-4a = these things). *Ina* arranges "these things" into an order based on producing greater joy, and this telic-extent identifies the greatest of these. You can see that telic-extents let *ina* B identify a term in A (like *toutōn*) while projecting to a telic end (having an order with no time sequence).

Rev. 13:13: *He performs great signs,* **so that** *he even makes fire come down out of heaven to the earth in the presence of men.* *Ina* B in v. 13 is not a sequential outcome of A, but shows how far "great signs" (A) can extend. So *ina* retains its telic meaning of showing "how great" – how far figuratively A can go – and B can also be a specific item in A.

Notice: in all 5 telic-extents, *ina* both identifies and projects to (telic) the greatest of a quality (how unworthy, God's love twice, things that bring joy, signs) – showing how far it can "figuratively go" or extend.

Every Ina in John's Writings Where the Telic May Be Easy-to-Miss

The spiritually informative verses (SIV's) in Chapters 1-6 typically have unclearly identified terms in *ina*'s A that help translators choose the "*ina* as if it were *oti*" option. Their use of this option in all of John's writings shows me that they consider it "less than ideal but not-so-bad". Chapter 7 and Apx. 3 show that this option is far worse than usually is assumed, causing both misinformation and the loss of vital information shown in the Scriptures in Chapters 1-8. Chapter 8 should help us see that this bad option is not needed – did John ever use it?

This section's group is every "easy-to-miss" telic of John's *ina's*. I judge all *ina*'s in this list as an easy-to-miss telic: John 1:27, 4:34, 5:36, 6:29, 6:39-40, 8:56, 9:22, 13:18, 13:29, 13:34, 15:8, 15:12-13, 15:16, 15:17, 15:25, 17:3, 17:11, 17:20-23, 18:37;   1John 3:1, 3:8, 3:11, 3:23, 4:21; 5:3, 5:16; 2John 5-7; 3John 4; Rev. 13:13, 13:17, 14:13. Here I discuss all underlined verses in their contexts. Any verse not underlined is discussed on the pages in the list below. (I apologize if I omit an *ina* that you think belongs on this easy-to-miss list).

John 1:27, 3John 4, Rev. 13:13 (the telic-extents): p. 100-101
John 4:32-34: p. 12-14
John 5:36: p. 65, 75
John 6:28-30: p. 14-17
John 6:37-40: p. 76
John 8:56: p. 77
John 9:22: p. 66, 78
John 13:29: p. 81-82 (repeated on p. 131-132 and 140)
John 13:34: p. 21-23, 46 (in 1John 4:12-17 discussion)
John 15:8, 12, 13, 16, 17: p. 24-26
John 17:11, 20-23: p. 30-32, 85-86, 133 (I judge 5 of 7 *ina*'s hard-to-see)
John 18:37: p. 87, 134
1John 5:16: p. 47
2John 5-7: v. 5-6 are on p. 47-49; v. 6-7 are on p. 138 and 67 (17:24).

Often *ina*'s A is hard-to-see because of an unidentified term (like "this") in A. This section can help us see that valid A's are little or large, and easy-to-miss or even implied (as in John 13:18 and 1John 3-5).

John 13:18: *I do not speak of all of you. I know the ones I have chosen;* *b**but it is that [ina] the Scripture may be fulfilled, "He who eats My bread has lifted up his heel against Me."* Here A is not written but is easy to know. From John 12:4-6 and 13:2, 10-11, 21-30 and v. 18a, A is the disciple Judas being among them: he was not truly following Jesus and for a while was intending to betray Him (John 12:4, 13:2, and 13:27). John 17:12 confirms this A. Judas' being among them (source A) produced the outcome B: fulfilling the Scripture quoted in v. 18 (He who eats My bread...). The need to identify an unwritten (implied) A in v. 18 with a clearly valid solution in a very large context can be an example to encourage us to realize that a true A might not be easy to identify or not be clearly stated, as with the other 38 *ina*'s (identified on p. 102) that are often thought to act like *oti*.

John 15:24-25: [24]*If I had not done among them the works which no one else did, they would not have sin; but now they have both seen and hated Me and My Father as well.* [25]*But they have done this to [ina] fulfill the word that is written in their Law, "They hated Me without a cause."* "They have done this" is not in the Greek, but is inserted by the translator to represent their hating Jesus and God shown in v. 24. V. 25 is useful for this section, because v. 25 shows an "*ina* B" with an "easily identified but easy-to-miss in Greek" A, the source of B. V. 24 (their hating Jesus) was *ina*'s source A for its outcome B: to fulfill the quoted Scripture (literally, in order that the word may be fulfilled...).

John 17:2-3: [2]*even as You gave Him authority over all flesh, that to all whom You have given Him, He may give eternal life.* [3]*This is eternal life, that [ina] they may know You, the only true God, and Jesus Christ whom You have sent.* *Ina* and know (*ginōskō*) in v. 3 are discussed with John 17:3 on p. 29-30. Here we discuss the antecedent to "This" in v. 3, which I see as v. 2, but for a different reason than all other "this...*ina*" verses. I write the next paragraph with an invitation for readers who know Greek to correct an important mistake.

Notice the v. 2 transition to v. 3: "...He may give eternal life. [3]This is eternal life ina..." The crucial Greek is "eternal life autē de is eternal life", where *de* is a connective. In Perschbacher's *The New Analytical Greek Lexicon* that I have relied on for its information, he says that "*de*" often "marks the superaddition of a clause": here v. 3 would be the "over and above" feature of "eternal life" that Jesus put into this context of v. 2. Therefore I see this underlined transition from v. 2 to *ina* in v. 3 as the "telic source A" that sets up the "they may know You..." as a key outcome B of eternal life, and "This" in v. 3 is incidental instead of very important to a telic source-outcome A *ina* B meaning.

I refer you to p. 35-42 for a foundation for all of the 1John *ina*-verses. HERE I ADD relevant preceding verses to those on p. 35-47 to show a telic *ina*'s hard-to-see antecedent A or a very relevant "this" in A. 6 of the following verses in 1John 3-5 have helped many excellent translators to assume that John may use *ina* like *oti*.

1John 2:28-3:1: *²⁸Now, little children, <u>ABIDE IN HIM</u>, <u>so that</u> when He appears, we may have confidence and not shrink away from Him in shame at His coming. ²⁹If you know that He is righteous, you know that everyone also who practices righteousness is born of Him. ³:¹<u>See how great a love</u> the Father has bestowed on us, ᵇthat [**ina**] we would be called children of God; and such we are. For this reason the world does not know us, because it did not know Him.* I quote 2:28-3:1 to show the "1John commandment" that applies throughout 1John 3-5, but v. 28 specifically is part of a "larger source A" for *ina* in 1John 3:1.

The Father's great love bestowed on us (a nearby source A) <u>leads to this outcome</u>: we are called His children: clearly telic and true. <u>What is a special way</u> to see His great love? 2:28 commands us to abide (stay) in Him, a short way to <u>identify the fellowship in Jesus</u> in <u>1:1-4 and</u> in <u>all of 1John</u> that Jesus commanded in John 15:4, 9-10. <u>Abiding in Him</u> helps us <u>see and experience</u> His great love. (Both A's fit *ina*'s A → B).

His <u>great love given to us</u> <u>is so great</u> that we could be called children of God (*ina*'s B), and John affirms we are. 1John 3:1's telic-extent is seen with John's other 4 telic-extents on p. 100-101; 2 helpful features in 3:1 are on p. 60, 110; and 3:1's fullest discussions are on p. 44, 89.

1John 3:5-8: *⁵You know that <u>He appeared</u> **in order to** [**ina**] <u>take away sins</u>; and in Him there is no <u>sin</u>. ⁶No one who <u>abides in Him</u> <u>sins</u>; no one who <u>sins</u> has seen Him or knows Him. ⁷Little children, make sure <u>no one deceives you</u>; the one who <u>practices righteousness</u> is righteous, just as He is righteous; ⁸ᵃthe one who <u>practices sin</u> is of the devil; for the devil has <u>sinned</u> <u>from the beginning</u>. The <u>Son of God appeared</u> for <u>this purpose</u>, ⁸ᵇ**to** [**ina**] <u>destroy the works of the devil</u>.* Here I repeat (p. 45) my comment on v. 5-8. The best choice I see for A of v. 8's *ina* is "<u>our sin and its removal</u>" in <u>v. 5-8a</u>: Jesus appeared to <u>take away sins</u> (v. 5); no one who abides in Him <u>sins</u> (v. 6: keeps sinning, Greek present tense); and the one <u>practicing sin</u> is of the devil, who sinned from the beginning (v. 8a). 1John 3:<u>5-8a</u> is <u>a large antecedent A</u> and is "<u>this purpose</u>". <u>He appeared</u> <u>so that He could produce these OUTCOMES</u>: <u>TAKE AWAY SINS</u> (v. 5), and <u>DESTROY the WORKS of the devil</u> (v. 8).

Both outcomes <u>include the sins of people who sin</u>. V. 6-7 show that <u>CONTINUED sin</u> <u>disrupts our abiding in Jesus</u>, and this fits into John 15:5-6: to choose to disconnect from Him for a sin can <u>dry up abiding fellowship with Him</u>. If God speaks to a believer, <u>refusing</u> God or His voice <u>can disrupt his/her abiding life in Christ</u>. V. 5-8 with a telic *ina* in v. 8 show that <u>Jesus' taking away sins</u> <u>and</u> <u>OUR turning from sins</u> (not staying in them) are <u>keys to destroying the works of the devil</u> (the devil's real goal and work is to separate people from God, and tempting people to sin is a key way).

1John 3:11: *For this is the message which you have heard from the beginning, that [ina] we should love one another.* A telic meaning of v. 11 is easy to see if we realize, When is "the beginning"? V. 11's "the beginning" is near the beginning of each believer's true fellowship with God in all 1John (p. 40). As v. 11 shows, initial 1John receivers heard a message then that led to this outcome: loving one another. What is v. 11's "message heard from the beginning"? To abide (stay) in Jesus, a short way to say: "stay in this special fellowship in Him" that 1John describes and 1John 2:28 reminds (p. 35-42). So 1John 3:11 concisely REMINDS believers to stay in this fellowship with God and His true children, and they could understand this reminder. V. 11 before *ina* is its source A that should lead into this outcome B: loving one another.

1John 3:22-24: *²²and whatever we ask we receive from Him, because we keep His commandments and do the things that are pleasing in His sight. ²³This is His commandment, that [ina] we believe in the name of His Son Jesus Christ, and love one another, just as He commanded us. ²⁴The one who keeps His commandments abides in Him, and He in him. We know by this that [oti] He abides in us, by the Spirit whom He has given us.* As explained on p. 35-42, the single commandment is to abide in Him in 1John 2:28: it is a distant context of 3:23, but 3:24 immediately follows v. 23 with a brief reminder about abiding in God – evidence that 2:28's command to abide in Him is still meaningfully connected to 3:23-24, and that John expected initial 1John receivers to know well what His commandment meant. Abiding in Jesus (staying in this life-giving fellowship shown at the start of 1John) will produce key OUTCOMES: we believe in the name of God's Son Jesus Christ and love one another, just as He commanded us elsewhere. John did not miscount 1 instead of 2, or did not add the second commandment as an afterthought. (We consider "this" before *oti* in 3:24 with 4:9 below).

1John 4:9: *By this the love of God was manifested in us, that [oti] God has sent His only begotten Son into the world so that [ina] we might live through Him.* "We might live through Him" (*ina*'s B) is a desired outcome of *ina*'s A (God sending Jesus into the world): *ina*'s A → B.

   4:9 and 3:24 both illustrate John's use of *oti* B to identify its A that includes this, a poorly identified word (p. 60-61). *Oti*'s B in 4:9 (God sent Jesus so that we might live through Him) identifies "this" and a specific manifestation of God's love in us (both are in *oti*'s A). In 3:24 "by God's Spirit" (in *oti*'s B) identifies "by this" and the way we know He abides in us. 1John 4:9 and 3:24 are examples of John using *oti* in its normal way to do what translators often assume is a way he used *ina*.

1John 4:12-17: *¹²...bif we love one another, God abides in us, and His love is perfected in us. ¹³By this we know that we abide in Him and He in us, because [oti] He has given us of His Spirit.* [14]*We have seen and testify that the Father has sent the Son to be the Savior of the world.* [15]*Whoever confesses that Jesus is the Son of God, God abides in him, and he in God.* [16]*We have come to know and have believed the love which God has for us. God is love, and the one who abides in love abides in God, and God abides in him.* [17]*By THIS, love is perfected with us,* **so that** *[ina] we may have confidence in the day of judgment; because as He is, so also are we in this world.* V. 12b-17 are explained on p. 46. Here I identify 1 great meaning of v. 17's THIS using 3 good contexts. One antecedent-source is the abiding fellowship in v. 16b; a second is the 4 abide statements in v. 12-16, and a third is all of 1John with its inclusive 1John commandment to abide in Him in 1John 2:28.

1John 4:18-5:1: [18]*There is no fear in love; but perfect love casts out fear, because fear involves punishment, and the one who fears is not perfected in love.* [19]*We love, because He first loved us.* [20]*If someone says, "I love God," and hates his brother, he is a liar; for the one who does not love his brother whom he has seen, cannot love God whom he has not seen.* [21]*And this commandment we have from Him,* **that** *[ina] the one who loves God should love his brother also.* [5:1]*Whoever believes that Jesus is the Christ is born of God, and whoever loves the Father loves the child born of Him.*

  In this section you can read 1John 4:12b-5:3 (almost together) to see a lack of an explicit commandment for 4:21 in v. 12b-21 and also see the emphasis on abiding in the fellowship with God and one another in Jesus. 4:20 makes clear: truly loving God always includes loving one's brother. And 5:1 shows that a command in 4:21, "love his brother also", has no use here: if I truly love God, then I do love my brother, His child. 1Tim. 1:9 confirms v. 21's lack of command: a law is made for potential violators and not for those who always do what it says. The Greek also confirms: "should love" (v. 21) and "loves the child" (5:1) are *agapa* – either indicative or subjunctive, but NOT the commanding imperative *agapatō*. Instead, 4:21's true command ("abide in Jesus") is throughout its specific context and all 1John, and obeying this command will lead to 4:21's telic *ina* outcome B: loving God and his brother also.

1John 5:2-3: [2]*By this we know that we love the children of God, when we love God and observe His commandments.* [3]*For this is the love of God,* **that** *[ina] we keep His commandments; and His commandments are not burdensome.* God's love (*ina*'s A) is the source of the outcome that we keep His commandments: *"We love, because He first loved us"* (1 John 4:19, above, underlined); and *"If anyone loves Me, he will keep My word"* (John 14:23). As explained on p. 111, "His commandments are not burdensome" more likely connects with "we keep His commandments", but is also a result or outcome of His love.

A good antecedent for "this" as v. 3 begins might <u>not be obvious to us</u>, but can be identified. All of 1John and <u>this specific section of it</u> <u>(4:7-5:3)</u> emphasizes the <u>loving, life-giving fellowship</u> with God and His children (the <u>initial 1John receivers</u> are <u>treated like they know it well</u>). It provides two excellent meanings of "this": this fellowship, and 5:2's "<u>love God</u> and <u>observe</u> [*poieō*, do] His commandments" that are featured parts of this fellowship. Either meaning of "this" is <u>a part of the love of God</u> (A) that empowers us to keep all of His commandments.

Rev. 13:12-17: [12]*He <u>exercises</u> all the authority of the first beast in his presence. And he <u>makes</u> the earth and those who dwell in it to [**ina**] worship the first beast, whose fatal wound was healed.* [13]*He <u>performs</u> great signs, **so that** [**ina**] he even <u>makes</u> fire come down out of heaven to the earth in the presence of men.* [14]*And he deceives those who dwell on the earth because of the signs which it was given him to <u>perform</u> in the presence of the beast, telling those who dwell on the earth to <u>make</u> an image to the beast who had the wound of the sword and has come to life.* [15]*And it was given to him to give breath to the image of the beast, **so that** [**ina**] the image of the beast would even speak and **<u>cause</u>** [ina?] as many as do not worship the image of the beast to be killed.* [16]*And he <u>causes</u> all, the small and the great, and the rich and the poor, and the free men and the slaves, **to** [**ina**] be given a mark on their right hand or on their forehead,* [17]*and he provides **that** [**ina**] no one will be able to buy or to sell, except the one who has the mark, either the name of the beast or the number of his name.* (<u>Some texts</u> have *ina* after v. 15's "cause": with or without *ina*, the "cause..." is a source-outcome statement, so that *ina* there adds little).

On p. 95 we see how each *ina* in v. 12-17 can easily be telic. Here we see v. 12-17 as a unit in order to see the large antecedent for the *ina* in v. 17. "he provides" (as v. 17 begins) is not in the Greek: v. 17 starts with, *"and so that no one could buy or sell except..."* In Greek, v. 17 is "and-*ina*-outcome" and shows more of what the second beast would make, do, or cause (all <u>8 underlined words</u> from v. 12 to early v. 16 are *poieō*). Therefore we see that v. 17 really is a telic *ina* B with *ina*'s A spread out over v. 12-16, and the NAS probably <u>inserted "he provides"</u> to consolidate <u>*ina*'s large antecedent A</u>.

Rev. 14:13: *And I heard a voice from heaven, saying, "Write, '<u>Blessed are the dead who die in the Lord from now on!'"</u> "<u>Yes</u>," <u>says the Spirit</u>, "**so that** [**ina**] they may rest from their labors, for their deeds follow with them."* B (after *ina*) is clearly an outcome, but A is easily missed. I see "the blessing with the Spirit's affirmation of it ('Yes')" before *ina* as a good source A of outcome B (they may rest...) – a telic A *ina* B.

Consistently *Contingent* Verbs in Ina B: Subjunctives, With 13 Possible Future Indicatives

This section is only for those who want or need further evidence of John's consistent *ina-oti* distinction. As Chapters 1-8 show, John's Gospel and 3 Epistles contain all of his SIV's (spiritually informative *ina*-verses). John's consistent use of a subjunctive verb in B in his Gospel and 3 Epistles (171 *ina*'s) is one more huge way to see that he consistently did not use *ina* as if it were *oti*: his *oti* B normally has an indicative B-verb. An outcome normally is contingent until it is fulfilled, but contingency has no part or function in identifying a specific A.

We first review (p. 56-57) the key issue for this section. The Greek subjunctive mood has a special function: to express that its idea is not yet a fact, but is an "if" that is contingent on its fulfillment. I quote from Zodhiates' *Key Word Study Bible* (#43 in grammatical definitions): "The *Subjunctive Mood* makes an assertion about which there is some doubt, uncertainty, or indefiniteness. It is closely related to the future tense, which helps point up the fact that often the uncertainty only arises because the action has not yet occurred." The subjunctive mood is specifically distinguished from the indicative mood ("The *Indicative Mood* makes an assertion of fact": Zodhiates #24) and the imperative mood ("The *Present Imperative* is a command to do something in the future and involves continuous or repeated action": Zodhiates #37). Notice two ways to express contingency vs. a present fact of a present indicative: a subjunctive, and a future indicative as a "not-yet-fully-fact".

John's telic *ina*'s predominantly produce an outcome (3 telic-extents have a telic "end" as an extent), so that a future indicative tense B with another tense A is consistent with B being not yet a fact: a contingency now. Because a future indicative is closely related to the subjunctive and implies contingency by unfulfilled action, I conclude that a future indicative *ina*-B verb instead of a subjunctive should not disturb the conclusion that John clearly distinguished *oti* from his telic *ina*. If you also conclude this, then you do not need to read the next 6 pages.

You should read the rest of Apx. 1 if you believe my conclusion is wrong or I received bad information from my Greek sources. I am not a Greek scholar and you might have better sources of Greek, but as you can see in the next 6 pages, my sources show me that John never used a future indicative B-verb definitely inconsistent with a purely telic *ina* with its source-outcome relationship. After we see the hard cases, on p. 114 I shall again conclude: John's contingent *ina*-B-verb is consistently different from his factual indicative *oti*-B-verb.

{ If you want to know my primary sources of Greek, I use: Marshall's *Interlinear NASB / NIV New Testatment* (1993) that is based on Nestle's 21st Edition, and Pershbacher's *The New Analytical Greek Lexicon* (1990, 2006). I also use *Key Word Study Bible* (Zodhiates), Wigram and Winter's [Greek] *Word Study Concordance* (or its 1999 update, Wigram's *The Englishman's Greek Concordance of the New Testament*), and the *NAS Exhaustive Concordance.* }

My Greek sources show only 1 out of 171 *ina* B's in John's Gospel and 3 Epistles as maybe inconsistent with a subjunctive. We consider John 7:3, even though both the subjunctive and future indicative texts fit with an outcome (contingent!) that might not yet be a fact.

John 7:3: *...Leave here and go into Judea,* **so that** *Your disciples also may see Your works which You are doing.* Perschbacher shows 3 texts as future indicative and 2 as subjunctive, so I call this "text-dependent": this makes it NOT a definite example of John using a non-subjunctive-B-verb in his Gospel or 3 Epistles. And the commands to Jesus in *ina*'s A are telic and contingent: they are given to set up His disciples seeing His works IF He will obey these commands from His brothers, but they realize that He might not obey their commands.

With the other 170 *ina*'s, I find every *ina*-B-verb can be subjunctive. With all 171 *ina*'s in John's Gospel and 3 Epistles, I call *ina*'s B-verb "always contingent" and "consistently" subjunctive. John normally used a factual indicative after *oti* unless *oti*'s A or B had its own cause: examples are John 11:56 (p. 142), or 1John 1:6 starting its A with "if", which caused its B-verb to also be contingent (p. 58, 139). His consistent subjunctive *ina*-B-verb for contingency strongly confirms that John CLEARLY DISTINGUISHED *INA* FROM *OTI* in all 171 *ina*'s.

This section is completed except for those who want to consider these 5 footnotes that end Apx. 1, which I put in slightly smaller font.

1. Some verbs have the same spelling for the tense and person of the factual indicative, the contingent subjunctive, and/or the commanding imperative (a command must remove contingency to be a full command instead of a request). A key example is the 2nd person plural present tense *agapate* for "love" – all three moods! Any such verb allows all of its meanings and cannot be used to distinguish one allowed meaning from another.

2. On p. 141-146 I provide a thorough report of checking the mood of the B-verb for every *ina and oti* in John 11-17. My brief report is that all 75 *ina*'s can be subjunctive, and the 1 *oti*-subjunctive-B-verb (John 11:56) out of 94 *oti*-B's was in a question that emphasized the answer was not a fact. The statement itself caused the subjunctive – *oti* did not cause it. Therefore John 11-17 clearly illustrates John's thorough distinction in his use of *ina* and *oti*.

3. John's consistently contingent (subjunctive) B-verbs in his Gospel and 3 Epistles confirms the purely telic *ina* and may give us further insight into 3 specific verses:

John 15:8: *My Father is glorified by this,* **that** *you* bear *much fruit, and so prove to be My disciples.* "Bear" is subjunctive and "prove" is future indicative in my text. If one accepts "subjunctive verbs in *ina* B", this difference shows that *ina*'s B stopped with fruit, and *"so prove to be My disciples"* is connected to *"bear much fruit"*.

1John 3:1a: *See how great a love the Father has bestowed on us,* **that** *we would be called children of God; and such we are.* The NAS translates well the verbs after *ina*: "would be called" is subjunctive and in *ina* B, but "we are" is indicative: John affirms B is a fact. John ERASED the CONTINGENCY that normally is contained in his SUBJUNCTIVE. This also demonstrates John was sensitive to his *ina*-subjunctive-verb normally showing contingency.

1John 5:3: *For this is the love of God, **that** we keep His commandments; and His commandments are not burdensome.* This comment is like the other two (p. 110): "keep" is subjunctive and "are" is present indicative. If we realize that John was careful about subjunctive verbs in *ina* B, *"His commandments are not burdensome"* is truly connected to *"we keep His commandments"* instead of *"love of God"* (but here either connection gives a good truth: p. 91, 106).

4. On p. 56 we saw how the NAS's 1John 3:8 gives no hint of the contingent subjunctive *ina lusē* (to destroy in the NAS), which is subjunctive aorist and is not indicative or infinitive or any other *luō*. John 4:34 also illustrates the relevant Greek moods: *"[34]Jesus said to them, 'My food is **to do** [ina poiō] the will of Him who sent Me and to [no ina, but inserted well from the first ina] **accomplish** [teleiōsō] His work.'"* In this context, "to do" and "to accomplish" give no hint of a contingent subjunctive. The contingency in the present subjunctive or future indicative *teleiōsō* fits well into v. 34's *ina* B as a contingent outcome instead of identifying what Jesus' food is. "To do" *poiō* is both present indicative and present subjunctive, but *teleiōsō* highly favors *poiō* as subjunctive over indicative. This fits well into v. 34's *ina* B as a contingent outcome instead of identifying what Jesus' food is.

5. This is the final footnote that will complete Apx. 1. Revelation has 12 *ina*-B's with a subjunctive-future indicative issue like John 7:3 (p. 109), so that here in #5 we can see each verse. This lets you see explicitly how these possible future indicative verbs fit well with *ina*'s telic source-outcome, and see good reasons for this section to separate Revelation's 12 possible non-subjunctives from the 171 *ina*'s in John's Gospel and 3 Epistles.

Consider features of Revelation's 12 *ina* B's that cause them to differ from John's other *ina*'s (here we consider only for this section's topic):

1. In every "exception" in Revelation, John quoted a prophetic word that he was hearing from Jesus or another source with God's authority, so that this was not John's choice of words nor his option to change any word.

2. As God provided the prophetic word, Jesus or the voice from heaven has all authority and power to remove all contingency from a statement that is not yet a fact but will definitely be fulfilled in the future.

3. Instead of writing a prophecy from the resurrected Jesus or "from heaven", John's Gospel is his Spirit-inspired narrative (quotes of Jesus are most likely translated into Greek) and each brief Epistle was his Spirit-inspired letter – not his quoting exactly what he heard.

4. My sources of Greek text rarely agree about these subjunctive vs. future indicative verbs, even though they usually agree about other issues (only John 7:3 [p. 109] of John's 171 *ina* B's in his Gospel and 3 Epistles have this problem). So much confusion in 12 verses over what seems to me as a minor issue helps me to regard Revelation's *ina*'s as special in this issue.

Below are all 12 *ina* B's in Revelation with possible future indicatives but also being different from the 171 *ina*'s in John's Gospel and 3 Epistles:

Rev. 3:9: *Behold, I will cause those of the synagogue of Satan, who say that they are Jews and are not, but lie – I will make them* [**ina**] *come and bow down at your feet, and make them know that I have loved you.* Ina is not translated in v. 9: its A *ina* B part says, *"I will make them (A) so that they shall come and shall bow down at your feet and shall know that I have loved you"* (B is after "so that"). 7 of my 8 sources (my Greek sources minus Zodiates plus 1977 and updated NAS, ESV, and KJV) show future indicative verbs in B. V. 9 is not John's words: he is quoting Jesus, so that John did not choose the verbs. I believe that the Lord Jesus intentionally removed all contingency out of this Scripture for the future of v. 9's A, even while their "coming and bowing down…" is clearly an outcome (telic) of what Jesus will make them do.

Rev. 3:11: *I am coming quickly; hold fast what you have,* **so that** *no one will take your crown.* My Greek text and 3 others show *labē*, the subjunctive (contingent) that could be translated "may take" but not "will take", and none of my 7 sources imply a non-contingent B for *ina*. "Holding fast to what they have in order that no one take their crown" is a telic source-outcome A-B and a contingent B with either a subjunctive or a future indicative verb in B.

Rev. 6:4: *And another, a red horse, went out; and to him who sat on it, it was granted to take peace from the earth, and* **that** *men would slay one another; and a great sword was given to him.* In Rev. 6:4, 6:11, 9:4, 9:5b, and 14:13, Perschbacher shows the Majority Text and the Received Text have the B-verb (would slay) as subjunctive, but three other texts as future indicative. Translations normally vary as subjunctive, future indicative, or the ambiguous "that" or "to". "Men slay one another" clearly is an outcome of source A: "he on the red horse" was granted permission to take peace from the earth.

Rev. 6:11: *And there was given to each of them a white robe; and they were told* **that** *they should rest for a little while longer, until the number of their fellow servants and their brethren who were to be killed even as they had been, would be completed also.* As in Rev. 6:4 above, "rest" as subjunctive vs. future indicative depends on the text. The aorist "were told" fits into their resting longer as a projected outcome in the future of whatever they were told.

Rev. 8:3: *Another angel came and stood at the altar, holding a golden censer; and much incense was given to him,* **so that** *he might add it to the prayers of all the saints on the golden altar which was before the throne.* Perschbacher and my Greek text show future indicative, but you see the subjunctive 1977 and Updated NAS translations (the KJV also is subjunctive while the ESV and

RSV write the ambiguous "to"). "Much incense was given" (aorist) is source A that precedes the intended future outcome B: he adds this to the saints' prayers (so 8:3 is also clearly telic).

Rev. 9:4: *They were told **not to** <u>hurt</u> the grass of the earth, nor any green thing, nor any tree, but only the men who do not have the seal of God on their foreheads.* As in Rev. 6:4 above, "hurt" is text-dependent. The aorist "were told" is the source A that precedes and is clearly intended to produce the future outcome B: hurting only the unsealed men.

Rev. 9:5: *And they were **not** permitted **to** <u>kill</u> anyone, but **to** <u>torment</u> for five months; and their torment was like the torment of a scorpion when it stings a man.* My Greek text shows "to kill" as subjunctive and "to torment" as future indicative. Like in 8:3, translations for both verbs vary, and others cover the issue with "to". Even with many text-dependent possibilities, what the locusts were given or permitted (A) was to <u>prevent</u> the <u>possible future outcome</u> B of killing someone but to <u>allow the outcome</u> B of tormenting people for 5 months.

Rev. 9:20: *The rest of mankind, who were not killed by these plagues, did <u>not repent</u> of the works of their hands, **so as not to** <u>worship</u> demons, and the idols of gold and of silver and of brass and of stone and of wood, which can neither see nor hear nor walk.* My Greek text has a future indicative, Zodhiates has an aorist subjunctive, translations vary, and Perschbacher does not list the Greek text word for repent. Regardless of a lack of grammatical clarity and confirmation (which helps me to separate John's Revelation *ina*'s from his 171 other *ina*'s in his Gospel and brief Epistles for only this section), <u>B's contingency and *ina*'s telic meaning are clear</u>: not repenting of the works of their hands would cause the rest of mankind to continue their worship of demons and idols, but <u>repenting</u> (<u>changing A</u>) <u>would change this outcome</u>.

Rev. 13:12: *He exercises all the authority of the first beast in his presence. And he makes the earth and those who dwell in it ᵇto <u>worship</u> the first beast, whose fatal wound was healed.* Like 9:20, my Greek text has a future indicative, Zodhiates has an aorist subjunctive, and most translations avoid this issue with "to" (as in the NAS). The telic *ina* projecting into a future outcome is again clear despite lacking grammatical confirmation: the second beast makes (Greek present tense with its continued action) those dwelling on earth to worship the first beast – an intended outcome in the future of v. 12a. The exception of the 144,000 (Rev. 14:3) proves 13:12's contingency.

Rev. 14:13: *And I heard a voice from heaven, saying, "Write, '<u>Blessed</u> are the dead who die in the Lord from now on!'" "<u>Yes</u>," <u>says the Spirit,</u> "**so that** they <u>may rest</u> from their labors, for their deeds follow with them."* As in Rev. 6:4 in this list, "rest" is text-dependent. The Spirit saying (the ongoing present tense) "Yes" to the blessing is *ina*'s source A that precedes the projected outcome B: their resting from their labors.

Rev. 18:4: *I heard another voice from heaven, saying, "Come out of her, my people, **so that** you <u>will</u> **not** <u>participate</u> in her sins and [ ] <u>receive</u> of her plagues.* The contingency and telic *ina* are clear: coming out of her (source A) is to prevent an outcome of participating in her sins and receiving her plagues. The NAS did not translate the "*ina* not" before "receive", but instead let the first "so that" carry over to the not "*receive of her plagues*". {Here I add that the updated NAS in v. 4 is the only future indicative among my major sources. The updated NAS changed the subjunctive to a future indicative in 16 other John-*ina*-verses. I conclude that this is a part of its move away from increasingly obsolete English like Thee, Thou, ye, lest, and subjunctives. Therefore if the updated NAS is the only indicator I have of a future indicative, then I do not regard this as a true indicator of an indicative: I expect the Greek text is likely to be a subjunctive B-verb. But I checked even these verses for being telic and a contingent B, and I see no problem with a purely telic *ina* and a consistent *ina-oti* difference in the B-verb.}

The above verses are the only possible future indicatives I find. I remind you of my more explicit report on p. 141-146 for this section's statements with all *ina*'s and *oti*'s in John 11-17. A better knowledge of Greek and/or better Greek sources could help any analysis, so that I submit my findings to such people. I hope that I made my examination sufficiently clear that they, you, or anyone can check if I missed anything crucially important to this confirmation of John's purely telic *ina* provided by his consistently using subjunctive B-verbs in his Gospel and 3 Epistles (171 *ina*'s), and to the confirmation of this distinction from possible exceptions in Revelation. (I hope to help anyone seeking the truth about John's *ina* to correct, confirm, or add to what I did).

With these 171 *ina*'s, John reliably used a contingent verb (subjunctive) after *ina* and an indicative verb after *oti* (unless the *oti* statement contained its own contingency, an "if"). John's use confirms his telic-*ina*'s contingency and his careful *ina-oti* distinction – a truly huge confirmation because it allows so many opportunities for John to reveal a very clear exception. My finding only prophetic *ina*'s in Revelation that often varied with the choice of Greek text confirmed to me that these few exceptions should not disturb this confirmation from abundant evidence of a consistently contingent subjunctive verb after *ina* in John's Gospel and 3 Epistles. Moreover, we saw again that none of these exceptions challenged John's use of a purely telic *ina* everywhere.

Appendix 2

All of John's *Oti*-Verses

This whole book is about John's use of a purely telic *ina*. Chapter 8 shows a telic meaning for each *ina*: why do we need to know about *oti*? As Chapters 1-7 show, for centuries excellent translators translated *ina* B as if it identified like *oti* B in 22 spiritually informative verses (SIV's) in John's Gospel and 3 Epistles. If a verse is very <u>informative</u>, then we <u>often lack confirmation</u> of the information supplied there. With 171 *ina*'s in John's 4 books and 42 more in Revelation, any reader may not believe some of the new explanations (indeed, I can expect that some people will give better explanations for some telic *ina*'s in John). Therefore we can benefit from realizing that the <u>assumption</u>, "John sometimes used *ina* B to identify A like *oti* B", does not agree with his consistent and careful distinction of *ina* and *oti* in his extensive use of each. We discuss this in Chapter 7 and Apx. 3.

Sections 1-2 of Apx. 2 are written to put on record my analysis of *oti* for anyone who wants to check it. Section 3 and Chapter 7 provide 80 examples of *oti*'s two basic meanings: "identify specifically" and "because". The final Section 4 of Apx. 2 shows all 12 *oti*'s in John that are not in the form A *oti* B, so that anyone can see none of these exceptions affects any conclusion I made about *oti* (and *ina*). I often express a conclusion in the predominant (97%) A *oti* B form in order to state it clearly, accurately, unambiguously, and as simple as it is.

Each section in Apx. 2 is written only for those who want or need it. READ ONLY AS MUCH AS you want or need to know the truth God wants you to know about John's verses that use *ina* and *oti*. To help you decide, I identify the purpose of each section in Apx. 2 in its title or at its beginning, and I add a conclusion at the end of Section 3.

1: Every Oti-Verse in John Grouped by
Meaning and Relationship to Oti's A

I count 234 times that John used *oti* B to identify *oti*'s A. In "say *oti* B" as an "A *oti* B", B identifies what was specifically said (in contrast to *ina*'s desired or projected outcome of what was said); in "know *oti* B", B identifies what is known relevant to an issue A out of all the person knows. A is a "big category", and B is a specific item in the category. The 9 underlined *oti*'s in the list are discussed on p. 58-59.

John 1:20 1:32 1:34 1:50b 2:17 2:22 3:2 3:11 3:19 3:21 3:28ab 3:33 4:1ab 4:17 4:19 4:20 4:21 4:25 4:27 4:35ab 4:37 4:39 4:42ab 4:44 4:47 4:51 4:52 4:53 5:6 5:15 5:24 5:25 5:32 5:36 5:42 5:45 6:5 6:14 6:15 6:22ab 6:24 6:36 6:42 6:45-46 (clarify A in v. 45) 6:61 6:65 6:69 7:7b 7:12 7:22 (clarify A) 7:26 7:35 7:42 7:52 8:17 8:24ab 8:27 8:28 8:33 8:34 8:37a 8:48 8:52 8:54 8:55 9:8 9:9ab 9:11 9:17b 9:18 9:19 9:20ab 9:23 9:24 9:25 9:29 9:30 9:31 9:32 9:35 9:41 10:7 10:34 10:36a 10:38 10:41 11:6 11:13 11:20 11:22 11:24 11:27 11:31ab 11:40 11:41 11:42ab 11:50 11:51 11:56 12:9 12:12 12:16 12:19 12:34ab 12:50 13:1 13:3ab 13:11 13:19 13:21 13:29 13:33 13:35 14:10 14:11 14:20 14:22 14:28ab 14:31 15:18 15:25 16:4a 16:15 16:19a 16:20 16:26 16:27b 16:30ab 17:7 17:8bc 17:21 17:23 17:25 18:8 18:9 18:14 18:37 19:4 19:10 19:21 19:28 19:35 20:9 20:13 20:14 20:15 20:18 20:31 21:4 21:7 21:12 21:15 21:16 21:17ab 21:23ab 21:24 1John 1:5 1:6 1:8 1:10 2:3 2:4 2:5 2:18ab 2:19 2:22 2:29ab 3:2a 3:5 3:14a 3:15 3:16 3:19 3:20ab (1 identify, 1 clarify) 3:24 4:3 4:9 4:10ab (both clarify) 4:13a 4:14 4:15 4:20 5:1 5:2 5:5 5:9b 5:11 5:13 5:14 5:15ab 5:18 5:19 5:20   3John 12   Rev. 2:2 2:4 2:6 2:14 2:20 2:23 3:1ab 3:9 3:15 3:17bc 10:6 12:12b 12:13 16:5 17:8 18:7b [234 = 173 Gospel + 43 Epistles + 18 Rev.] 234 / 413 = .567   57%   *oti* B identifies A

B identifies a "this" in A that has no antecedent before A (* are quoted on p. 60-61, ** are on p. 136-137, and all 13 *oti*'s are in the above list):
John 9:30* 21:23a*   1John 1:5* 2:3* 3:16* 3:24** 4:9** 4:10ab 5:9b 5:11   Rev. 2:6* 2:14*

Oti ambiguous (both "identify" and "because" provide "good meanings" to the verse – all 19 are discussed in section 3, p. 119-123):

John 2:25* 3:7* 3:21 4:35b 8:44b* 10:17* 11:15* 13:35 16:9* 16:10* 16:11* 16:19 20:13 1John 3:16 3:20 4:9 5:9b Rev. 2:14 8:11* [10 are in the "identify" list and the other 9 * in the "because" lists]

In A *oti* B, *oti* means <u>because</u>, but is often shortened to a causal "for"; *oti* B shows a reason why A (the 4 underlined are explained on p. 62):

John 1:15 1:17 1:30 2:18 2:25 3:7 <u>3:18</u> 3:23 4:22 5:16 5:18 5:27 5:28 5:30 5:38 5:39 6:2 6:26ab 6:37-38 6:41 7:1 7:7a 7:8 7:23 7:29 7:30 7:39 8:14 8:16 8:20 8:22 8:29 <u>8:37b</u> 8:43 8:44ab <u>8:47</u> 9:16 9:17a 9:22 10:4 10:5 10:12-13 10:17 10:26 10:33 10:36b 11:9 11:10 11:15 11:47 12:6ab 12:10-11 12:18 12:39 12:41 12:48-49 14:2 14:12 14:17ab 14:19 14:28c 15:5 15:15ab 15:21 15:27 16:3 16:4b 16:9 16:10 16:11 16:14 16:19b 16:21ab 16:27a 16:32 17:7-8a 17:9 17:14 17:24 18:2 18:18 19:7 19:20 1John 2:8 2:11 2:12 2:13ab 2:14abc 2:15-16 2:21abc 3:1 3:2b 3:8 3:9ab 3:10-11 3:12 3:14b 3:22 4:1 4:4 4:7 4:8 4:13b 4:17 4:18 <u>4:19</u> 5:3-4 5:6 5:6-7 5:9a 5:10 2John 4 2John 7 Rev. 3:4 3:8 4:11 5:4 5:9 6:16-17 7:16-17 8:11 11:2 11:10 11:17 12:10 12:12a 13:4 14:7 14:15ab 14:18 15:1 15:4abc 16:6 16:21 17:14 18:2-3 18:4-5 18:8 18:10 18:11 18:16-17 18:19 18:20 18:23ab 19:1-2,2 19:6 19:7 21:4 21:5 22:5

[167 = 89 Gospel + 36 Epistles + 42 Rev.]

All 11 *oti*'s with the exceptional form *oti* B A have *oti* = because. To this group I add the 12th exceptional *oti*, John 16:17*, where the disciples' quoted only the *oti* B part of Jesus' statement in 16:10. All 12 are in section 4, p. 124-126.

John 1:16 1:50a 8:45 15:19 16:6 16:17* 19:42 20:29 Rev. 3:10 3:16 3:17a-18 (first-*oti*: B=v.17, A=v.18) 18:7b-8a (first-*oti*: B=7b, A=8a). [12=8+0+4]

(167+12=<u>179</u>) / 413 = .433 43% *oti* = because, *oti* B shows why A

B identifies "<u>this</u>" in A of "A because B" (all 3 are in the A because B list and both * are discussed on p. 60-61): John 8:47* 1John 3:1* 4:13b

2: John's Normal Use of Oti to Show "Outcome ← Cause":
Reversing the Flow of Ina's Source → Outcome Relationship

On p. 63 I stated my conclusion about the 179 times John used *oti* = because (*oti*'s A ← B):

"I find over 140 in which <u>A as the outcome</u> or <u>B as the source</u> seems very clearly specified by the context or situation or sequence, far fewer that are not as clear, about 25 in which either A or B could be the cause (without further analysis), and <u>zero</u> (none) that flows like a telic *ina*: in the telic *ina*'s A → B, <u>A</u> is <u>a source of</u> an "outcome" B. 140+ to 0 in the <u>very clear uses</u> is utterly <u>consistent</u>! I identify every judgment-call in Apx. 2."

This quoted conclusion shows one <u>big</u> way that John carefully and consistently used *ina* (A → B) and *oti* (A ← B) differently.

The previous section identified the 179 *oti* = because (167 A *oti* B's, 11 *oti* B A's, and 1 partial quote). Here are the verses where I judged A as a <u>very clear</u> outcome and/or B a <u>very clear</u> cause (a kind of source):

John 1:15 1:16 1:17 1:30 1:50a 2:18 3:7 3:18 3:23 5:16 5:18 5:27 5:28 5:30 5:39 6:2 6:26ab 6:37-38 6:41 7:1 7:7 7:8 7:23 7:29 7:30 7:39 8:14 8:16 8:20 8:22 8:43 8:45 8:47 9:16 9:17 9:22 10:12-13 10:33 10:36b 11:9 11:10 11:15 11:47 12:6ab 12:10-11 12:18 12:39 12:41 12:48-49 14:12 14:19 14:28c 15:15ab 15:19 15:27 16:4b 16:6 16:10 16:11 16:14 16:19b 16:21ab 16:32 17:14 17:24 18:2 18:18 19:7 19:20 19:42 20:29　　　1John 2:11 2:12 2:13ab 2:14abc 2:15-16 2:21abc 3:1 3:8 3:9b 3:12 3:14 3:22 4:1 4:4 4:7 4:8 4:17 4:18 4:19 5:10　　　2John 4　　　Rev. 3:4 3:8 3:10 3:16 3:17-18 4:11 5:4 5:9 6:16-17 7:16-17 11:2 11:10 11:17 12:10 12:12a 13:4 14:7 14:15ab 14:18 15:1 15:4abc 16:6 16:21 17:14 18:2-3 18:4-5 18:7b-8 18:8 18:10 18:11 18:16-17 18:19 18:20 18:23ab 19:1-2 19:2 19:6 19:7 21:4 21:5 22:5

[75 in John's Gospel + 26 in Epistles + 45 in Revelation = 146 of "<u>very clearly</u> A is an outcome <u>or</u> B its source": 146 is the 140+]

To help those interested in checking my judgments, in the next 3 lists I identify the primary reason that I judged the A or B "very clearly" an outcome or cause: the <u>situation provides a sequence</u>, A is <u>very clearly the outcome</u>, or B is <u>very clearly the cause (a source)</u>. Many A *oti* B's have 2 or 3 of these reasons. (To prevent counting the same *oti* twice, I mark a verse with a * if it is in a list above it, and I subtract it so that it is not counted again: for example, all except 1John 5:10 in the third list.)

Situational sequence: John 1:15 1:30 1:50a 2:18 3:7 3:18 5:16 5:18 5:27 6:2 6:26ab 6:41 7:23 7:29 7:39 8:22 9:16 9:17 9:22 10:33 10:36b 11:15 11:47 12:6ab 12:10-11 12:18 12:39 12:41 12:48-49 15:27 16:6 16:10 16:11 16:19b 16:21b 17:24 18:2 19:7　　　1John 2:12 2:13ab 2:14abc 2:21abc 3:1 3:14b 4:1 4:17　　　Rev. 3:4 3:8 3:10 3:16 3:17-18 4:11 5:4 5:9 11:10 11:17 12:10 12:12a 14:18 18:2-3 18:4-5 18:7b-8 18:20 18:23ab 19:1-2,2 19:7 21:4　　(76)

B clearly a cause: John 1:16 1:17 1:50a* 3:7* 3:23 5:16* 5:18* 5:28
5:30 5:39 6:38 7:1 7:7 7:8 7:29* 7:30 8:14 8:16 8:20 8:43 8:45
8:47 9:16* 9:22* 10:12-13 11:9 11:10 11:47* 12:48-49* 14:12
14:19 14:28c 15:15ab 15:19 15:27* 16:4b 16:14 16:21a 16:32
17:14 18:18 19:7* 19:20 19:42 20:29   1John 2:11 2:15-16 3:8
3:9b 3:12 3:22 4:4 4:7 4:8 4:17* 4:18 4:19 2John 4   Rev. 3:8*
3:10* 3:16* 3:17-18* 4:11* 6:16-17 7:16-17 11:2 13:4 14:7
14:15ab 15:1 15:4abc 16:6 16:21 17:14 18:2-3* 18:4-5* 18:7b-8*
18:8 18:10 18:11 18:16-17 18:19 18:20* 19:1-2*,2* 19:6 21:5 22:5
(92 − 23* = 69) [76+69+1 = 146 are <u>very clear</u> source A or outcome B]

A clearly an outcome: John 1:50a* 3:7* 7:23* 8:43* 9:22* 10:33*
10:36* 11:15* 12:39* 16:21* ,21*   1John 2:21* 3:12* 3:14* 5:10
Rev. 3:16* 3:17-18* 18:2-3* 18:7b-8* 19:1-2*,2* (21 − 20* = 1)

3: John's 19 Oti's That Can Both Identify A and Show Why A

I use <u>all</u> 19 *oti*'s that I believe show both meanings of *oti* to provide

fresh examples of how John used *oti*. You should be able to see John's

use of *oti* B to <u>identify A</u> and also to <u>show why A</u>. In contrast, I see the

other 394 *oti* B's as far more one than the other. You can also see what *ina*

B's telic outcome would do to each verse: <u>introducing *ina* in place of *oti* into 19 contexts</u>

that allow both meanings of *oti* can help you see <u>how</u> *ina* and *oti* provide very different

meanings and are poorly <u>exchangeable</u>. (This combines with other demonstrations in

Chapter 7 and Apx. 3. I put this "*ina* in place of *oti*" in reduced font-size so that you can

easily separate this from the *oti* meanings).

John 2:24-25: *But Jesus, on His part, was not entrusting Himself to
them, for He knew all men, *[25]*and **because** (**oti**) He did not need
anyone to (ina) testify concerning man, for He Himself knew what was
in man. Oti in v. 25 can* show why *Jesus was* not entrusting Himself to
men *(A in "A because B": B = He had no need for testimony about man
for* He knew *what was* in *man). But *oti* can* also identify A*, where A is
"*knowing all men*" and B specifies *that with no testimony He knew what
was IN man. Ina in place of oti could* fit well here *with v. 24's "Jesus knowing all
men" as ina's source A. Its outcome of "He did not need anyone to testify about man
for He knew what was in man" is true, but not what v. 25 says with its oti.*

John 3:7: *Do not be amazed **that** [oti] I said to you, "You must be born
again".* Jesus identified what amazed Nicodemas, showed why he was
amazed, and told him to not be amazed. B as telic *ina*'s outcome cannot fit
here because B was repeating Jesus' statement made in v. 3, which had amazed
Nicodemas (we see another repeat in John 16:19).

John 3:21: *But he who practices the truth comes to the Light, so that [ina] his deeds may be manifested ᵇas [oti] having been wrought in God.* Having been wrought in God (*oti*'s B) <u>identifies</u> what his deeds manifest (A). Being wrought in God (B) causes the deeds to manifest <u>their Source</u> and, in a larger A for *oti* (v. 20-21a), causes some to come to the Light: A ← B for the *oti* = because. A telic *ina* in place of *oti* would have shown that the manifested deeds (A) would lead to or produce the end result that they were wrought in God – against v. 21, which has God as a Source of the deeds.

John 4:35b: *Do you not say, "[oti] There are yet four months, and then comes the harvest"? Behold, I say to you, lift up your eyes and look on the fields, that [oti] they are white for harvest.* The bold *oti* B <u>both identifies</u> what they see when they look on the fields and <u>shows why</u> they should lift their eyes to look on the fields. A telic *ina* (so that) in place of the bold *oti* would show the fields being white for harvest as an outcome of looking at them: lift up your eyes and look on the fields so that they are white for harvest. This spiritual nonsense illustrates again how *ina* and *oti* are not freely interchangeable.

John 8:44b: *You are of your father the devil, and you want to do the desires of your father. He was a murderer from the beginning, and does not stand in the truth because [oti] there is no truth in him. Whenever he speaks a lie, he speaks from his own nature, for [oti] he is a liar and the father of lies.* The bold *oti* B both identifies a specific feature of the devil's nature and shows why he lies. A telic *ina* instead of the bold *oti* would show that speaking from his nature would produce the outcome of his being a liar. This is true, but not what this Scripture says with its *oti*.

John 10:17: *For this reason the Father loves Me, because [oti] I lay down My life so that I may take it again.* <u>Both meanings of *oti*</u> in v. 17 can <u>fit well</u>: because is usual, but I believe identify is better. V. 17 shows a good reason why Father God loves Jesus. But other verses (John 17:24 is one) show that the Father's love for Jesus preceded His laying down His life and taking it up, so that I do not think v. 17 is the normal *oti* = because statement. Better: His laying down His life <u>identifies</u> a specific lovable feature of Jesus that His Father loves. IF *ina* were used in place of *oti*, then we <u>could</u> see a Biblical outcome (1John 4:19), but not what v. 17 says with *oti*. (<u>IF</u> John <u>possibly</u> used *oti* like *ina*, then we should consider if v. 17 shows the truth in 1John 4:19: we love, because God first loved us).

John 11:15: *and I am glad for your sakes that [oti] I was not there, so that [ina] you may believe; but let us go to him.* *Oti*'s B (I was not there so that you may believe) both <u>identifies</u> what Jesus was glad about for them and (I believe to be better) <u>shows why</u> He was glad for them. "I am glad for you so that I was not there" (*ina* in place of *oti*) is <u>not</u> Jesus' way or love.

John 13:35: *By this all men will know that [oti] you are My disciples, if you have love for one another.* The usual translation of *oti* is good ("*oti* = that" identifies what all men will know out of all they will know). What is easily missed is that *oti* = because is also good. His disciples loving one another <u>would cause</u> this outcome: people know that they are His disciples. *Ina* in place of *oti* puts "what men know" as a source of discipling: bad!

John 16:9: *concerning sin,* **because** *[oti] they do not believe in Me.* John's use of *oti* B to identify A can fit v. 9-11 in addition to the usual translation of "because". Not believing in Jesus (B) is a deadly sin that causes the Spirit's conviction A (so that the usual translation is good), but notice how "not believing in Jesus" identifies a specific key sin for conviction. *Ina* in place of *oti* in v. 8-11 reverses each source-outcome relationship: *ina* in v. 9 would show that sin caused their not believing in Jesus. This is a Biblical truth found in John 3:18-20, but is not what 16:9 says with its *oti*.

John 16:10: *and concerning righteousness,* **because** *[oti] I go to the Father and you no longer see Me.* Jesus' going to the Father and out of their sight identifies a righteous judgment that would prevail first for Jesus but also for those in the world who receive the Spirit's conviction (v. 8). *Oti*=because explains that Jesus is going to the Father <u>in order to</u> <u>send the Holy Spirit</u>, with the <u>outcome</u> that He convicts the world of God's righteousness (A ← B). *Ina* in v. 10 would show Holy Spirit's conviction of the world about righteousness as a source of Jesus' going to the Father and out of the disciples' sight – putting a false reaction onto God and reversing the true sequence of Jesus sending the Spirit (16:7). The v. 7-11 context rules out *ina* and bad lies here.

John 16:11: *and concerning judgment,* **because** *[oti] the ruler of this world has been judged.* The ruler of this world has been judged specifically identifies this key issue out of all of the issues about judgment. *Oti*=because can show the increased conviction of people about judgment by God's Spirit (outcome B) because the world's ruler has been judged and defeated (A ← B). *Ina* in v. 11 would reverse the stated time sequence in v. 7-11, putting "the ruler of the world <u>has been judged</u>" (previous) as <u>an outcome</u> of Jesus sending the Holy Spirit to convict the world that would "begin" within 2 months: *ina* in place of *oti* in v. 11 is incompatible with the v. 7-11 context.

John 16:19: *Jesus knew that [oti] they wished to question Him, and He said to them, "Are you deliberating together about this, that [oti] I said, 'A little while, and you will not see Me, and again a little while, and you will see Me'?"* <u>Identifying specifically what</u> the disciples deliberated about and <u>showing why</u> they were deliberating (because I said...) fit very well. A telic *ina* (so that) in place of *oti* is incompatible with the context: what Jesus had said previously (in 16:16) could not be an outcome of what they were currently deliberating (as we also see in John 3:7 about 3:3's born again).

John 20:13: *And they said to her, "Woman, <u>why</u> are you weeping?" She said to them, "**Because** [oti] they have taken away my Lord, and I do not know where they have laid Him."* *Oti* = because and *oti* identifying the answer to the question are <u>good, compatible meanings</u> of *oti* in v. 13: "<u>because</u>" <u>is an optional part of the reply</u> if asked "why" –

it is implied if not stated explicitly. *Ina* again cannot be used in place of *oti*: her weeping was not a source of their taking Jesus' body away.

1John 3:16: *We know love by this,* ***that*** *[oti] He laid down His life for us; and we ought to lay down our lives for the brethren.* Jesus' laying down His life for us (*oti*'s B) especially identifies both "this" and our truly "knowing love". And His laying down His life for us is very much a cause or source of our knowing love (A ← B for *oti* = because). *Ina* (so that) in place of *oti* creates sequential nonsense and unnecessary spiritual ambiguity.

1John 3:19-20: [19]*We will know by this that [oti] we are of the truth, and will assure our heart before Him* [20]*in whatever [oti] our heart condemns us;* ***for*** *[oti] God is greater than our heart and knows all things.* The usual translation of "for=because" for the bold *oti* is excellent: "God is greater than our heart and knows all things" (B) is the cause and source of our assuring our heart before Him when it condemns us (A), and also is the way to assure our hearts. But "God is greater than our heart and knows all things" (B) also clarifies and further identifies our being of the truth while assuring our heart before Him when it condemns us (A): He is always right and in truth (but not in lies), but our heart is not always either one. A telic *ina* (so that) in place of this *oti* cannot work here: *oti*'s B must be the source of truth and cannot be an outcome.

1John 4:9: *By this the love of God was manifested in us,* ***that*** *[oti] God has sent His only begotten Son into the world so that [ina] we might live through Him.* "God sending Jesus into the world so that we may live through Him" (B) specifically identifies this and His love manifested in us (A), and also is the cause or source of His love manifested in us (A ← B again for *oti* = because gives a truth like 1John 4:19). *Ina* instead of *oti* could almost fit into v. 9 (with a John 3:16 meaning and God's love produced in us believers), but the "love of God manifested in us" causes a sequential contradiction if *ina* were used instead of *oti*: Jesus came before His love in us.

1John 5:9b: *If we receive the testimony of men, the testimony of God is greater; for [oti] the testimony of God is this,* ***that*** *[oti] He has testified concerning His Son.* You can see how God's testifying about His Son (B) identifies God's testimony and "this", but probably you can also see how we can RECEIVE God's greater testimony (also in A) because He has testified concerning His Son (source B, A ← B). And you can see that God's testifying concerning Jesus came before our receiving it, so that His testifying about Jesus is not an outcome: *ina* in place of *oti* does not fit v. 9.

Rev. 2:14: *But I have a few things against you,* ***because*** *[oti] you have there some who hold the teaching of Balaam, who kept teaching Balak to put a stumbling block before the sons of Israel, to eat things sacrificed to idols and to commit acts of immorality.* *Oti*'s B is v. 14-15 after *oti*. You can understand this *oti* B as reasons or causes to be against this church, or this *oti* B can specifically identify the few things against this church (which I believe fits God's nature better: He is not truly against a real church). Using *ina* in place of *oti* again creates spiritual nonsense: Jesus having a few things against them (A) as a source of their sins is nonsense ("...have a few things against you so that you have..." inverts God's justice).

Rev. 8:11: *The name of the star is called Wormwood; and a third of the waters became wormwood, and many men died from the waters,* **because** *[oti] they were made bitter.* You can see that "many men died from the waters, <u>because</u> they were made bitter", but you can also see that "many men died from the waters <u>that</u> were made bitter" also makes total sense (B <u>identifies</u> a key feature of these waters). You can further see that many men died from the waters as the source of their becoming bitter (*ina* in place of *oti*: many men died from and in the waters so that they became bitter) is a very different picture – possible (could occur in a situation), but not the true v. 11.

These 19 *oti*'s provide 38 examples of *oti*'s two basic meanings in 19 contexts (plus 6 *oti*'s needing no discussion). This adds to 36 other *oti*'s discussed in Chapter 7, to 28 *oti*'s shown in *ina*-verses and other SIV's in Chapters 3-6, to 17 more *oti*'s in the next section, plus Apx. 3.

We also see that replacing *oti* with *ina* in 19 contexts produces variable results, and this can show us much. I judged 14 of 19 (about 3/4) contexts incompatible with switching *oti* and a telic *ina*. This is a useful insight: *oti*'s two meanings fit all 19 contexts, but about 3/4 of the contexts were incompatible with *ina*'s telic meaning. This lets us see clearly that these 19 contexts are <u>restrictive</u>: not allowing almost any meaning of a conjunction to fit.

The other 5 (about 1/4) are also instructive, because inserting *ina* in place of *oti* <u>created</u> 2 Biblical truths (John 10:17, 16:9), 2 reasonable truths (John 2:25, 8:44), and a reasonable possibility (Rev. 8:11). This shows that introducing *ina*'s meaning into an *oti*-context makes understanding John's Scriptures more complicated, and this can help us realize that <u>freely interchanging *ina* and *oti*</u> is a <u>huge</u> <u>assumption</u>.

Apx. 4 shows how <u>assuming</u> "John <u>may use</u> *ina* to identify as *oti*" affects the content of <u>each *ina*-verse</u> in John's Scriptures. Apx. 4 is not in your book, but I intend to send it to those who ask for this further evidence of John's consistently telic *ina*. (Ask jamesmtarter@aol.com.)

4: Seeing No Effect Produced by All 12 Exceptions
to John's Use of the Form A Oti B

On p. 99-100 we saw all 5 *ina*'s that were not in the form A *ina* B. With all 5 *ina*'s, you could see that re-writing the Scripture in the form A *ina* B did not change the source-outcome relationship of A and B. In this section you get to see the same lack of change in all 12 of John's *oti*'s that are not in the form of A *oti* B: 11 are *oti* B A, and 1 is quoting only the *oti* B part of Jesus' statement. I first show the 1, then the 11.

John 16:10...17: *¹⁰and <u>concerning righteousness,</u> **because** [oti] <u>I go to the Father</u> and you no longer see Me.... ¹⁷Some of His disciples then said to one another, "What is this thing He is telling us, 'A little while, and you will not see Me; and again a little while, and you will see Me'; and, '**because** [oti] <u>I go to the Father</u>'?"* John 16:9-11 is discussed on p. 121, where we see both "identify and because" meanings of *oti* fit v. 9-11 well. Here we assume the more frequent translation of "because" in v. 10. When the disciples quoted Jesus in v. 17, they left off *oti*'s A and said only "*oti* B". Clearly this exception – a quote that ignored A in order to bring out B – does not affect John's other 412 uses of *oti*.

Now let us see all 11 *oti* B A's and their not affecting my outcome A ← source B statements about A and B (<u>a cause</u> is <u>one kind of source</u>).

John 1:16: **For** [oti] *of His fullness we have all received, and grace upon grace.* "For" is short for "because", "<u>of His fullness</u>" is <u>source B</u>, and "we have all received" is outcome A from His fullness B. You can see no change in the A–B relationship as I write this as A *oti* B: *"We have all received because of His fullness"* ["and grace upon grace" is another outcome we have all received from His fullness, this source B].

John 1:50a: *Jesus answered and said to him, "**Because** [oti] I said to you that [oti] I saw you under the fig tree, do you believe? You will see greater things than these."* Bold *oti*'s outcome A is "do you believe?", and source B is "I said to you that I saw you under the fig tree". Notice the lack of change in the A ← B outcome-source relationship as I put the Scripture in an A *oti* B form: *"Do you believe because I said to you that I saw you under the fig tree?"* As for all in this list, outcome A ← source B for *oti* = because in both forms.

John 8:45: *But **because** [oti] I speak the truth, you do not believe Me.* Again, notice the lack of change in the A–B relationship as I write the statement in A *oti* B form: *"But you do not believe Me because I speak the truth."* outcome A ← source B

John 15:19: *If you were of the world, the world would love its own; but* **because** *[oti] you are not of the world, but I chose you out of the world, because of this the world hates you.* *Oti*'s <u>long source B</u> is "you are not of the world, but I chose you out of the world"; "because of this" (a literal *dia touto*) is "*oti* B repeated in 3 words"; and *oti*'s outcome A is "the world hates you". Notice the lack of change in content or outcome-source relationship in A *oti* B: *"The world hates you because you are not of the world, but I chose you out of the world."*

John 16:6: *But* **because** *[oti] I have said these things to you, sorrow has filled your heart.* Notice the same A–B outcome-source relationship in the A *oti* B rewrite: *"But sorrow has filled your heart because I have said these things to you."*

John 19:42: *Therefore because of the Jewish day of preparation,* **since** *[oti=because] the tomb was nearby, they laid Jesus there.* Notice the same A–B outcome-source relationship in the A *oti* B rewrite: *"They laid Jesus there [in the tomb] since it was nearby."*

John 20:29: *Jesus said to him,* "**Because** *[oti] you have seen Me, have you believed? Blessed are they who did not see, and yet believed."* Notice the same A–B outcome-source relationship in the A *oti* B rewrite: *"Have you believed because you have seen Me?"*

Rev. 3:10: **Because** *[oti] you have kept the word of My perseverance,* [b]*I also will keep you from the hour of testing, that hour which is about to come upon the whole world, to test those who dwell on the earth.* Source B is "you have kept the word of My perseverance", and outcome A is v. 10b (I also will keep you...dwell on the earth). Notice the same A–B outcome-source relationship in the A *oti* B rewrite: *"I also will keep you from the hour of testing...dwell on the earth because you have kept the word of My perseverance."*

Rev. 3:16: *So* **because** *[oti] you are lukewarm, and neither hot nor cold, I will spit you out of My mouth.* Notice the same A–B outcome-source relationship in the A *oti* B rewrite: *"So I will spit you out of My mouth because you are lukewarm, and neither hot nor cold."*

Rev. 3:17-18: [17]**Because** *[oti]* [b]*you say,* "[oti] *I am rich, and have become wealthy, and have need of nothing," and you do not know that* [oti] *you are wretched and miserable and poor and blind and naked,* [18]*I advise you to buy from Me gold refined by fire so that you may become rich, and white garments so that you may clothe yourself, and that the shame of your nakedness will not be revealed; and eye salve to anoint* *your eyes so that you may see.* The bold *oti*'s source B is v. 17b (all of v. 17 after that *oti*), and its outcome A is all of v. 18. Notice the same A–B outcome-source relationship in the A *oti* B rewrite: *"[18]I advise you to buy from Me gold refined by fire so that you may become rich, and...and eye salve to anoint your eyes so that you may see, [17]because [b]you say, 'I am rich, and have become wealthy, and have need of nothing,' and you do not know that you are wretched and miserable and poor and blind and naked"* ("v. 18 *oti* v. 17b").

Rev. 18:7b-8a: *[7]To the degree that she glorified herself and lived sensuously, to the same degree give her torment and mourning; [b]for [oti] she says in her heart, "[oti] I sit as a queen and I am not a widow, and will never see mourning." [8]For this reason in one day her plagues will come, pestilence and mourning and famine, and she will be burned up with fire; [b]for [oti] the Lord God who judges her is strong.* The bold *oti*'s long source B is "she says in her heart, 'I sit as a queen and I am not a widow, and will never see mourning'", "For this reason" (*dia touto* to start v. 8) repeats *oti*'s source-B in 3 words, and its outcome is A: "in one day her plagues will come, pestilence and mourning and famine, and she will be burned up with fire" (in v. 8a).

Notice the same A–B outcome-source relationship in the A *oti* B rewrite: *"In one day her plagues will come, pestilence and mourning and famine, and she will be burned up with fire for [= because] she says in her heart, 'I sit as a queen and I am not a widow, and will never see mourning.'"* (The conclusions from v. 7b-8a are not affected by including v. 8b [God the Judge is strong] as <u>a second source</u> of the outcome A: her sudden judgment. Expressing these conclusions would be longer and less transparent if I had included the *oti*-source in Rev. 18:8b, which does add neatly to the emphasized *oti*-source B.)

Again, outcome A ← source B for *oti* = because in both forms for all in this list.

Appendix 3

Comparing Entire Groups of John's Ina- and Oti-Verses

I have not hidden any of the challenges to establishing John's use of a purely telic *ina* and his consistently careful distinction of *ina* and *oti* in all of his Scriptures. But in order to help readers <u>learn</u> the truth about John's use of *ina* and *oti* in Chapter 7, I chose what I considered to be the <u>most illustrative Scriptures</u> to show ideas that need to be communicated. My choosing these Scriptures may help a reader see what I see, but they provide a systematic weakness for establishing the truth: I am choosing Scriptures with my agenda.

I write Apx. 1-3 to help readers go beyond this intrinsic weakness in parts of Chapter 7, to make it easier to check my analysis of *ina* by those who want to see how *ina* has a telic nature in <u>any</u> or <u>every</u> verse in John's writings. Apx. 1 forms <u>complete groups of *ina*-verses</u>. Apx. 2 shows my judgment of <u>every *oti*-verse</u> in John's writings, and illustrates the *oti* verses with two <u>groups containing every *oti*-verse</u> with the specified features. In Apx. 3 I use <u>relevant whole groups</u> of *ina*'s and *oti*'s to complete *ina-oti* comparisons: one started on p. 65-68 and one reported on p. 110. I also compare the frequent "say *ina* or say *oti*".

Every Verse in John's Scriptures That Uses Both Ina and Oti
in the Same Context

In this section we compare <u>every verse containing both *ina* and *oti*</u>, because this provides 42 contexts to make a <u>side-by-side comparison</u> of <u>John's use of both *ina* and *oti*</u>, and to <u>see a complete group of</u>

verses (plus 3 2-verse-units marked with an &) to check how <u>consistent</u> he was in <u>his distinct uses of both *ina* and *oti*</u>. This section lets us see clearly that John's *ina* B consistently has its telic outcome B meaning (A → B), and *oti* B has its two meanings: "identifying the preceding A" (no arrow) or "showing why A" in an "A because B" statement (A ← B).

This section completes the analysis started on p. 65-68. In order to help you check if my illustrative sample of *ina-oti* verses on p. 65-68 (1/3 of the whole group) is representative instead of severely distorting the picture provided by the whole group, I put a * before each Scripture quoted with its comments on p. 65-68 (the first is John 3:21 below). In this list below, comments added to * verses are in [brackets].

John 2:24-25: *But Jesus, on His part, was not entrusting Himself to them, for He knew all men,* [25]*and* **because** *(oti) He did not need anyone* **to** *(ina) testify concerning man, for He Himself knew what was in man.* Oti in v. 25 can <u>show why</u> Jesus was <u>not entrusting Himself to men</u> (A in "A because B": B = He had no need for testimony about man for <u>He knew what was in</u> man – *oti*'s A ← B). But *oti* B can <u>also</u> <u>identify</u> <u>A</u>, where A is "<u>knowing all men</u>" and <u>B specifies</u> that with no testimony <u>Jesus knew</u> what was <u>IN</u> man. Jesus did not need anyone (*ina*'s source A) to produce this outcome B: tell Him about mankind. *Ina*'s A → B.

* John 3:21: *But he who practices the truth comes to the Light,* **so that** *(ina) his deeds may be manifested* **as** *(oti) having been wrought in God.* Having been wrought in God (*oti*'s B) <u>identifies what</u> his deeds <u>manifest</u> (*oti*'s A). Being wrought in God <u>also</u> <u>causes</u> the deeds to manifest <u>their Source</u>: *oti*=because's A ← B (both meanings of *oti* fit v. 21). In a larger A for *oti*, v. 20-21a, *oti*'s B <u>causes</u> some to come to the Light. In contrast, coming to the Light (*ina*'s A) sets up this possible outcome: his deeds are manifested as wrought in God. *Ina*'s A → B.

* John 5:36: *But the testimony which I have is greater than the testimony of John; for the works which the Father has given Me* **to** *(ina) accomplish – the very works that I do – testify about Me,* **that** *(oti) the Father has sent Me.* "The Father sent Jesus" is *oti*'s B that <u>identifies</u> what was testified (*oti*'s A). The Father gave Jesus works (*ina*'s A) so that Jesus should do and accomplish them (*ina*'s intended outcome B: *ina*'s A → B). <u>After</u> being given each work, Jesus did it, and its specific testimony about Him was *oti* the Father sent Jesus.

* John 6:5: *Therefore Jesus, lifting up His eyes and seeing* **that** *(oti) a large crowd was coming to Him, said to Philip, "Where are we to buy bread,* **so that** *(ina) these may eat?"* "A large crowd coming to Jesus" (*oti's* B) <u>identifies specifically</u> (specifies) what Jesus saw (*oti's* A) out of all He saw. (Notice that a telic *ina* B – so that – cannot replace *oti* B in v. 5). Buying bread (*ina's* A) would set up this desired outcome: people eat (*ina's* A → B). ("People eating" is not a specific "buying bread", unlike *oti's* meaning of identifying a specific A.)

John 6:15: *So Jesus, perceiving* **that** *(oti) they were intending to come and take Him by force* **to** *(ina) make Him king, withdrew again to the mountain by Himself alone.* "The crowd's intention to come and take Him by force to make Him king" (*oti's* B) <u>identifies specifically</u> what Jesus was perceiving (*ginōskō*). The telic *ina's* "to" is again literally "so that they would". Their coming to take Him by force was in order to produce their intended outcome of making Him king (*ina's* A → B).

John 6:37-38: *All that the Father gives Me will come to Me, and the one who comes to Me I will certainly not cast out.* ³⁸*For* **(oti)** *I have come down from heaven, not* **to** *(ina) do My own will, but the will of Him who sent Me.* *Oti* B (v. 38) shows <u>why</u> and how A (v. 37) would be fulfilled. Jesus' coming from heaven to do His Father's will (*oti's* B) <u>caused the outcome (A) in v. 37</u>: all that the Father gives Jesus come to Him and He casts out none of them (*oti's* A ← B). The A *ina* B within v. 38 should be clear: Jesus came from heaven (A) so that He could do His Father's will (*ina's* outcome-B) instead of letting Jesus' human will interfere with that. His coming from heaven is a source preceding its outcome: what He did and not do on earth after coming (*ina's* A → B).

* John 7:23: *If a man receives circumcision on the Sabbath* **so that** *(ina) the Law of Moses will not be broken, are you* <u>angry with Me</u> **because** *(oti) I made an entire man well on the Sabbath?* Jesus showed those Jews who were rejecting Him: Is "I made an entire man well on the Sabbath" (*oti's* B) the real <u>cause</u> of their anger- (*oti's* A ← B)? *Ina's* telic A → B is also clear: they provided circumcision on the Sabbath (*ina's* source A) in order to produce *ina's* intended outcome B: not break the Law of Moses.

* John 9:22: *His parents said* <u>this</u> **because** *(oti) they were afraid of the Jews; for the Jews had already agreed* **that** *(ina) if anyone confessed Him to be Christ, he was to be put out of the synagogue.* Being afraid of the Jews <u>shows why</u> his parents said "<u>this</u> (= <u>v. 20-21</u>)": *oti's* A ← B. *Ina's* B (9:22 after *ina*) <u>logically</u> could be either the intended outcome from the agreement (*ina's* A → B) or identifying what was agreed. A <u>telic *ina* in v. 22</u> shows John's insight that <u>their agreement</u> was <u>for an</u>

intended outcome: to intimidate any person out of confessing Christ or to punish anyone who did. A telic *ina* displays their stealthy purpose in what they agreed: this shows how a telic *ina* adds an insight with an authority that may be lost if *ina* is sometimes non-telic (which "that" is).

John 10:17: *For this reason the Father loves Me,* **because** *(oti) I lay down My life* **so that** *(ina) I may take it again.* Both meanings of *oti* in v. 17 fit well, but I believe "identify" is the better meaning. The usual translation is "because", and v. 17 shows a good reason why Father God loves Jesus (*oti*'s A ← B). But other Scriptures (John 17:24 is one) show that the Father's love for Jesus preceded His laying down His life and taking it up, so that v. 17 is not the normal *oti* = because meaning. Instead, His laying down His life identifies a specific lovable feature of Jesus that His Father loves. A telic *ina* in v. 17 shows that His laying down His life would produce the outcome of His taking it again – a perfect fit for *ina*'s part of v. 17 (*ina*'s A → B).

John 10:38: *but if I do them, though you do not believe Me, believe the works,* **so that** *(ina) you may know and understand* **that** *(oti) the Father is in Me, and I in the Father.* *Oti*'s B (the Father is in Jesus and He in the Father) identifies specifically what they should come to know and understand (*oti*'s A: the aorist and present tenses of *ginōskō*). *Ina*'s A (believe Jesus' works) can help produce its projected outcome: the Jews (and we readers) come to know and understand that Jesus had the special John 15:4-10 fellowship with His Father (*ina*'s A → B).

John 11:15: *and I am glad for your sakes* **that** *(oti) I was not there,* **so that** *(ina) you may believe; but let us go to him.* *Oti*'s B (I was not there so that you may believe) both identifies what Jesus was glad about for them (A) and shows why He was glad for them. "So that" for *ina* rightly shows that "I was not there" would be a source of their future believing. As p. 67, 100 explain, *ina* and *oti* are rightly placed to make "I was not there" a source of both outcomes: *ina*-B (*ina* you may believe: A → B) and A-*oti*=because (I am glad for your sakes because: A ← B).

John 11:31: *Then the Jews who were with her in the house, and consoling her, when they* saw **that** *(oti) Mary got up quickly and went out, they followed her,* supposing **that** *(oti) she was going to the tomb* **to** *(ina) weep there.* Both *oti*'s identify specifically what the Jews saw or supposed. The common "*ina*-subjunctive verb" translated here as "to weep" has a context that lets "to" communicate a telic outcome (*ina*'s A → B), but in many contexts the translation "to" looks like an infinitive, which does not communicate the telic property of *ina*.

John 11:41-42: *So they removed the stone. Then Jesus raised His eyes, and said, "Father, I thank You* **that** *(oti) You have heard Me.* [42]*I* *knew **that** (oti) You always hear Me; but because of the people standing around I said it, **so that** (ina) [b]they may believe **that** (oti) You sent Me."* The 3 *oti* B's <u>identify</u> what was <u>specifically</u> known or believed, or a specific gift for which Jesus thanked His Father. The A *ina* B is translated well with "I said it (in v. 41)" as A and v. 42b as outcome B.

John 11:50: *nor do you take into account **that** (oti) it is expedient for you **that** (ina) one man die for the people, and **that** the whole nation not perish.* *Oti*'s B (v. 50 after *oti*) <u>identifies specifically</u> what "you" did not take into account out of all of the other things "you" did not take into account. A *ina* B (= ...expedient for you that the outcome be one man would die for the people and the whole nation not perish) shows clearly that this is a prophecy with <u>God's intended outcome B</u> (and Caiaphas' intent in the stated outcome differed from God's intent in it). The bold "that" with no *ina* is inserted by the NAS because "the whole nation not perish" is also part of *ina*'s B. In fact, v. 50's *ina* B continues into v. 52 with an additional outcome (God gathering together His scattered children into one) from this source in v. 50's *ina* B (Jesus dying for many people so that they do not perish).

John 12:9: *The large crowd of the Jews then learned **that** (oti) He was there; and they came, not for Jesus' sake only, but **that** (ina) they might also see Lazarus, whom He raised from the dead.* "He was there" is *oti*'s B that <u>identifies specifically</u> what the large crowd learned (*oti*'s A). The crowd came (*ina*'s source A) in order that they also might see Lazarus (*ina*'s desired outcome B and *ina*'s A → B).

John 13:1: *Now before the Feast of the Passover, Jesus knowing **that** (oti) His hour had come **that** (ina) He would depart out of this world to the Father, having loved His own who were in the world, He loved them to the end.* *Oti*'s B (His hour had come) <u>identified specifically</u> what Jesus knew for His situation out of all He knew (*oti*'s A). The <u>telic A *ina* B</u> shows "His hour had come" was *ina*'s source A for its outcome at that time: He will leave the world and go to His Father: A → B.

John 13:19: *From now on I am telling you before it comes to pass, **so that** (ina) when it does occur, you may believe **that** (oti) I am He.* *Oti* B <u>identifies specifically</u> what the disciples would believe: Jesus is "I am". Telling them before it happens was <u>intended to produce *ina*'s outcome B</u>: they would believe that Jesus is I am (*ina*'s source A → B).

John 13:29: *For some were <u>supposing</u>, because Judas had the money box, **that** (oti) Jesus was <u>saying</u> to him, "Buy the things we have need of for the feast"; or else, **that** (ina) he should give something to the poor.* *Oti*'s A is supposing, and its B is v. 29 after *oti* and <u>specifically identifies</u> two things they were supposing. A telic *ina* shows that Jesus might have <u>said a statement</u> to Judas <u>to produce the outcome</u> of giving to the poor. (The Bible never shows that Jesus told a disciple, "give something" or "just do something", but He said the specific thing to be given or done. Therefore <u>some disciples would not suppose</u> that Jesus told Judas, "You should give <u>something</u>".)

* John 14:31: *but* **so that** (*ina*) *the world may know* **that** (*oti*) *I love the Father, I do exactly as the Father commanded Me....* Jesus' love for His Father (*oti*'s B) <u>identifies specifically</u> what the world is to come to know (*oti*'s A) – as usual for *oti*. *Ina* in v. 31 is an "*ina* B A" statement: p. 99-100 show that <u>writing *ina* B before A</u> never affects John's telic meaning of *ina*, and v. 31 illustrates this fact. The content and source-outcome relationship of A with B is not changed if Jesus had said, "I do exactly as the Father commanded Me (A) <u>so that</u> the world may know that I love the Father (B)". This is A *ina* B with the same source and outcome as the Scripture: *ina*'s A → B.

John 15:24-25: *If I had not done among them the works which no one else did, they would not have sin; but now they have both seen and* <u>*hated*</u> *Me and My Father as well.* [25]*But they have done* <u>*this*</u> **to** (*ina*) *fulfill the word that is written in their Law, "*(**oti**) *They* <u>*hated Me*</u> *without a cause."* The <u>untranslated *oti*</u> <u>specifically</u> <u>identifies</u> what is written out of their whole Law that applies to this situation. "They have done this" (v. 25 before *ina*) is not in Greek, but the translator adds it to represent their hating Jesus and God shown in v. 24. V. 25 illustrates a poorly seen antecedent A, because this "*ina* B" has an "easily identified but easy-to-miss in the Greek" A, the source of B. V. 24 (their hating Jesus and God) is *ina*'s source A for its outcome B: to fulfill the quoted Scripture (literally, in order that the word may be fulfilled...).

* John 16:4: *But these things I have spoken to you,* **so that** (*ina*) *when their hour comes, you may remember* **that** (*oti*) *I told you of them. These things I did not say to you at the beginning,* **because** (*oti*) *I was with you.* V. 4 in the NAS shows all 3 key translations: a telic *ina* and *oti* with its 2 meanings. The first *oti*'s B <u>identifies specifically</u> what the disciples were to remember: Jesus had told them of these things. The second *oti* B <u>shows why</u> Jesus did not tell them these things at the beginning: "I was with you" (<u>cause B</u> of this <u>*oti*'s outcome A</u> in A ← B). In contrast to these two meanings of *oti* in John's writings, v. 4's *ina* is telic. Jesus spoke these things (*ina*'s source A) in order to set up <u>*ina*'s outcome B</u>: the disciples would remember that He told them these things when their hour of fulfillment did come (*ina*'s B in *ina*'s A → B).

John 16:30: *Now we know* **that** (*oti*) *You know all things, and have no need for anyone* **to** (*ina*) *question You; by this we believe* **that** (*oti*) *You* *came from God.* As usual, both *oti*'s <u>identify specifically</u> (specify) what the disciples were knowing or believing. *Ina*'s A → B is literally, "You... have no need (A) so that one should "question" (*erōtaō*) You." As p. 47 explains, this presumptive questioning is as if He did not already speak rightly. Jesus' disciples now know that He says everything rightly and does not need (A) anyone to ask Him to say it better (outcome B).

* John 16:32: *Behold, an hour is coming, and has already come,* **for** (**ina**) *you to be scattered, each to his own home, and to leave Me alone; and yet I am not alone,* **because** (**oti**) *the Father is with Me.* The Father being with Jesus (*oti*'s B) <u>shows why</u> He was not alone (*oti*'s A): A ← B. *Ina* again is the telic A → B: "an hour has already come" would quickly get an outcome prophesied for it: the disciples get scattered.

* John 17:20-21: *I do not ask on behalf of these alone, but for those also who believe in Me through their word;* [21]**that** (**ina**) *they may all be one; even as You, Father, are in Me and I in You,* [b]**that** (**ina**) *they also may be in Us,* **so that** (**ina**) *the world may believe* **that** (**oti**) *You sent Me.* You sent Me (*oti*'s B) <u>identifies</u> what the world should believe. Jesus' prayer in v. 20 is a source for the first *ina*'s B: an outcome of our being one as Jesus and the Father are one, or like the 11 being one in 17:11. This A and B are the next *ina*'s A: its B outcome is <u>our being "in Them"</u> (in the special fellowship in John 15:4-10, 14:20). This B with v. 20-21a is the third *ina*'s A: our being "in God" sets up its outcome, the <u>world believes</u> *oti* <u>Father God sent Jesus</u> (this *ina*'s B). All *ina*'s are A → B.

John 17:23: *I in them and You in Me,* **that** (**ina**) *they may be perfected in unity,* [b]**so that** (**ina**) *the world may know* **that** (**oti**) [c]*You sent Me, and loved them, even as You have loved Me.* *Oti*'s B (v. 23c) <u>identifies</u> what the world should specifically come to know (A). God's abiding presence and work in us and out of us (v. 22 with the first *ina*'s A in v. 23) would lead to this *ina*'s outcome B: our being perfected in unity. In turn, v. 22-23a lead to the final outcome B: the <u>world comes to know</u> *oti* <u>Father God sent Jesus</u> (as in <u>v. 21</u>) and <u>loves us like Him</u>.

* John 17:24: *Father, I desire* **that** (**ina**) *they also, whom You have given Me, be with Me where I am,* **so that** (**ina**) *they may see My glory which You have given Me,* **for** (**oti**) *You loved Me before the foundation of the world.*   This is re-worded from p. 67:   [The first *ina* illustrates a special feature of *ina* with verbs like desire, ask, agree, plan, and command. These verbs are often followed by *ina* to show the intended goal or outcome of what is desired, asked for... If *oti* followed any of these verbs, this usually would identify the specific desire, request...

The second *ina* shows A (being with Jesus where He is) setting up <u>outcome</u> B (seeing Jesus' glory): *ina*'s A → B. *Oti* shows the same outcome from the opposite direction (*oti*'s A ← B): the Father's love for Jesus before the foundation of the world (*oti*'s B) <u>is a source</u> of Jesus' glory that <u>preceded</u> the disciples <u>seeing it</u> (*oti*'s A).   In v. 24, "<u>see My glory</u>" is <u>an outcome</u> (*ina*'s B and *oti*'s A) <u>with each conjunction placed to show this relationship</u>: "A *ina* B *oti*=because C", or A → B ← C, where B is 1 outcome (see My glory) with its sources or causes A and C. { This same kind of "*ina*-*oti*-sandwich" is in 1John 4:17 (p. 137) and 2John 6-7 (p. 138). John 11:15 (p. 67, 100, 130) and 1John 3:10-11 (p. 136) are "A *oti*=because B *ina* C", or A ← B → C (2 outcomes A, C). }]

* John 18:8-9: *Jesus answered, "I told you **that** (**oti**) I am He; so if you seek Me, let these go their way,"* [9]*to (**ina**) fulfill the word which He spoke, "(**oti**) Of those whom You have given Me I lost not one."* "I am" is the first *oti*'s B that <u>identifies specifically</u> what Jesus told them. The [untranslated second] *oti* B <u>identifies specifically</u> what Jesus spoke. An expanded literal translation of the "*ina* B = to B" is "so that the word would be fulfilled…".   Jesus' command, "let these go", <u>led to *ina*'s outcome B</u>: fulfilling His word, "…I lost not one" (a telic A *ina* B: A → B).

John 18:37: *Therefore Pilate said to Him, "So You are a king?" Jesus answered, "You say correctly **that** (**oti**) I am a king. For <u>this</u> I have been born, and for <u>this</u> I have come into the world, **to** (**ina**) testify to the truth. Everyone who is of the truth hears My voice."* "I [Jesus] am a king" (*oti*'s B) <u>identifies specifically</u> what Pilate's question said to Jesus: the big group A of all that Pilate said correctly was specified in the key item B for their conversation. "To testify" is a short way to say, "in order that I may testify". A telic *ina* in v. 37 shows that "Jesus' birth and coming into the world destined to be a king" is the "this" and the source A for producing this outcome B: <u>with authority He could testify to the truth</u> (*ina*'s A → B).

John 19:4: *Pilate came out again and said to them, "Behold, I am bringing Him out to you **so that** (**ina**) you may know **that** (**oti**) I find no guilt in Him."* "Pilate finding no guilt in Jesus" (*oti*'s B) again <u>identifies specifically</u> what they should know (*oti*'s A). The telic *ina* again shows that *ina*'s B (they may know *oti* Pilate finds no guilt in Jesus) is the desired outcome of *ina*'s A (bringing Jesus out to them). *Ina*'s A → B

John 19:28: *After this, Jesus, knowing **that** (**oti**) all things had already been accomplished, **to** (**ina**) fulfill the Scripture, said, "I am thirsty."* As usual for *oti*, all things had already been accomplished <u>specifically identifies</u> what Jesus knew out of all He knew. V. 28 is another non-"A *ina* B": A is "Jesus said, 'I am thirsty'", and this source A set up this telic *ina*'s outcome B: fulfilling the Scripture (about His thirst). (As you can see on p. 99-100, re-writing all 5 of John's non- A *ina* B statements as A *ina* B does not affect the telic meaning of any *ina* or the basic content and source-outcome relationship of A to B: *ina*'s A → B).

John 19:35: *And he who has seen has testified, and his testimony is true; and he knows* **that** *(oti) he is telling the truth,* [b]*so that* *(ina) you also may believe.* *Oti*'s B (John is telling the truth) again specifically identifies what John knows out of all he knows. V. 35a (…truth) is *ina*'s A that sets up its outcome B: "you also may believe" (*ina*'s A → B).

John 20:31: *but these have been written* **so that** *(ina) you may believe* **that** *(oti) Jesus is the Christ, the Son of God; and* [b]*that* *(ina) believing you may have life in His name.* *Oti* B identifies what should be our belief out of all beliefs. The first *ina* shows that our believing the truth about Jesus was a desired outcome (goal) in John's writing his Gospel. The source A for the final *ina* is v. 31a (up to the *ina*), so that his writing and our believing about Jesus would lead to this desired outcome: with believing, we would have life in Jesus' name. Both *ina*'s are A → B.

* 1John 2:19: *They went out from us, but they were not really of us; for if they had been of us, they would have remained with us; but they went out,* **so that** *(ina) it would be* shown **that** *(oti) they all are not of us.* "They all are not of us" (*oti*'s B) identifies what was shown by their going out (*oti*'s A: v. 19 up to *oti*). *Ina*'s A (the leavers' going out from John's group) produced its outcome B: showing openly (manifesting) that they were not of John's group (true disciples). *Ina*'s A → B

The antecedents and sources for a purely telic *ina* in 1John are explained systematically on p. 35-42. There or p. 43-47 show more about most of the individual verses in 1John 3-5 below. Here I state the *oti* meaning and the telic *ina* meaning in each verse in 1John 3-5 that contains both *ina* and *oti*, and refer to the page(s) in Chapters 5-6 (p. 35-47) for a more thorough explanation of the telic *ina* in that verse.

1John 3:1: *See how great a love the Father has bestowed on us,* **that** *(ina) we would be called children of God; and such we are. For* this reason *the world does not know us,* **because** *(oti) it did not know Him.* The world not knowing the Father (*oti*'s B) identifies "this reason" in A and causes the world to not know us children of God (*oti*'s A: A ← B). The Father's great love bestowed on us leads to the outcome that we are called His children (*ina*'s A → B). V. 1 is further explained on p. 44 (or p. 104…), but we have fulfilled the purposes of this section for v. 1.

* 1John 3:5: *You know* **that** *(oti) He appeared* **in order to** *(ina) take away sins; and in Him there is no sin.* "He appeared in order to take away sins" (*oti*'s B) identifies specifically what "you know" (*oti*'s A) out of all you know. Taking away sins is *ina*'s B and is a major intended outcome of Jesus appearing on earth (*ina*'s source A). *Ina*'s A → B

1John 3:8: *the one who practices sin is of the devil;* **for** (**oti**) *the devil has sinned from the beginning.* [b]*The Son of God appeared for* this purpose, **to** (**ina**) *destroy the works of the devil.* Oti is "because": to see sin as a key practice of the devil (B) shows why "one who practices sin is of the devil" (*oti*'s A ← B). As explained on p. 45 or 104, the whole discussion of sin, its removal, and abiding in God in v. 4-8a is *ina*'s big single antecedent-source A and "this purpose" in v. 8. Jesus appeared in order to produce the outcome or result of destroying the works of the devil, which includes the sins of people who were sinning: *ina*'s A → B. (You can see that "He appeared *ina*" in v. 5 and 8 are closely related).

1John 3:10-11: [10]*By this the children of God and the children of the devil are obvious: anyone who does not practice righteousness is not of God, nor the one who does not love his brother.* [11]**For** (**oti**) *this is the* message *which* you *have* heard from the beginning, [b]**that** (**ina**) *we should love one another.* We consider v. 11's *oti* at the end. *Ina*'s true A is seen best in v. 11's context, all of 1John. I submit 2 Q&A: When would initial 1John readers first hear a message that would lead to the outcome of their loving one another? Near the beginning of his (her) life in Jesus (p. 40). What is v. 11's "message heard from the beginning"? To stay or abide in Jesus – a short way to say, "stay in this special fellowship in Him" that 1John describes and 1John 2:28 repeats (p. 35-42). So 1John 3:11 REMINDS believers to stay in this fellowship with God and His children: His New Commandment in John 15:4-12. V. 11a is *ina*'s A that should lead into its outcome B: loving one another. V. 11 is *oti* B and "shows why v. 10": *oti*'s A ← B. This message heard from their beginning (stay in Jesus) would lead to *ina*'s outcome (love...) and to *oti*'s outcome A in v. 10 (make children of God obvious). This *oti-ina* sandwich is "A *oti*=because B *ina* C", or A ← B → C (1 source: B).

& 1John 3:23-24: [23]*This is His commandment,* **that** (**ina**) *we* believe *in the name of His Son* Jesus *Christ, and* love one another, just as He commanded us. [24]*The one who* keeps His commandments abides in Him, and He in him. *We* know by this **that** (**oti**) *He* abides in us, by the Spirit *whom He has given us.* V. 23's telic *ina* is featured on p. 37-38: briefly, God's single command "abide in Him" includes the 2 commands to believe in Jesus and love one another, and doing this 1 command is a source of the outcome, fulfilling the other 2. V. 24 shows our abiding fellowship that includes keeping His commands is a key part of v. 23's context: "He abides in us" in *oti*'s B identifies what we know out of all we know. Also in *oti*'s B, "by His Spirit whom He has given us" identifies "by this" and shows how we know that we abide in this fellowship. { V. 23-24 are a 2-verse unit [like 2John 6-7 and Rev. 3:17-18] that I add to the 42 *ina-oti* single-verses because it is a key *ina-oti* unit whose *oti* is like 1John 4:9's *oti*. I also discuss *oti* B in 1John 3:24 and 4:9 together on p. 105, but its emphasis is to understand the "hard" *ina*'s. }

* 1John 4:9: *By* <u>this</u> *the* <u>love of God</u> *was* <u>manifested</u> <u>in us</u>, **that (oti)** *God has sent His only begotten Son into the world* **so that (ina)** *we might live through Him.* *Oti*'s B (= God sent Jesus into the world so that we might live through Him) <u>identifies</u> a specific manifestation of God's love <u>in</u> us and "<u>this</u>" (both are in *oti*'s A). "We might live through Him" (*ina*'s B) is clearly a desired outcome of *ina*'s source A (God sending Jesus into the world): *ina*'s A → B.

1John 4:16-17: *We have come to know and have believed the love which God has for us. God is love,* [b]*and the one who abides in love abides in God, and God abides in him.* [17]*By this,* <u>love is perfected with</u> <u>us</u>, **so that (ina)** *we may have confidence in the day of judgment;* **because (oti)** *as He is, so also are we in this world.* The *oti* "because" and the *ina* "so that" are translated well: *oti*'s B shows why we may have confidence in the day of judgment (*oti*'s A ← B). *Ina* is placed well to show <u>this same outcome</u> <u>from its other side</u>: God's love being perfected with us can give us confidence in the day of judgment (*ina*'s A → B, and 1 of 5 "*ina-oti* sandwiches" I show). As shown on p. 46 with Chapter 5, "this" that starts v. 17 can refer to the abiding fellowship in God in v. 16b, v. 12-16, and all of 1John, which fulfills the command in 1John 2:28 that is throughout 1John. As shown on p. 46, the greatest content in 4:16-17 is that <u>love is perfected in our abiding fellowship in</u> <u>God</u> (as we also concluded from John 13:34 and 15:4-17).

* 1John 5:13: *These things I have written to you who believe in the name of the Son of God,* [b]**so that (ina)** *you may know* **that (oti)** *you have eternal life.* *Oti*'s B (you have eternal life) <u>identifies specifically</u> *oti*'s A (what you may know) out of all that you may know. Knowing that you have eternal life (*ina*'s B) is an available outcome of both key parts of *ina*'s A: believing in the name of Jesus and John's writing to you believers. *Ina*'s A → B and *oti* B's identifying A fit again in 5:13.

1John 5:20: *And we* <u>know</u> **that (oti)** *the Son of God has come, and has given us understanding* **so that (ina)** *we may* <u>know</u> *Him who is true; and we are in Him who is true, in His Son Jesus Christ. This is the true God and eternal life.* *Oti*'s B extends up to *ina* and can extend through the end of v. 20 if that is true for the reader / hearer. *Oti*'s B <u>identifies specifically</u> (specifies) what we know (A) out of all we know. The first "know" is *oida*, to perceive fully or as a fact. The second is *ginōskō*: to "come to know increasingly" – especially experientially and relationally (p. 29). *Ginōskō* God and Jesus provides a fitting outcome B of His coming and giving us understanding (*ina*'s source A → B).

& 2John 6b-7a: *⁶ᵇThis is the commandment, just as you have heard from the beginning, **that** (**ina**) you should walk in it. **For** (**oti**) many deceivers have gone out into the world....* This *ina-oti* sandwich gives 2 sources for the outcome "you should walk in it" by *ina* and *oti* placed well (p. 67). P. 48 explains A *ina* B. *Oti*=because shows that many deceivers in the world is a cause for us to walk in Jesus according to His commands: doing this enables people to distinguish us clearly from the deceivers.

Rev. 3:9: *Behold, I will cause those of the synagogue of Satan, who say that they are Jews and are not, but lie – I will make them (**ina**) come and bow down at your feet, and make them know **that** (**oti**) I have loved you.* "I have loved you" (*oti*'s B) identifies specifically what God will make the others know (*oti*'s A). *Ina* B is a clear outcome of A (= I will make them), but *ina* is untranslated here to avoid the awkward English "make them to come and bow down", or the more awkward and more literal "make them so that they will come and bow down".

& Rev. 3:17-18: ***Because*** (***oti***) *ᵇyou say, "(**oti**) I am rich, and have become wealthy, and have need of nothing," and you do not know **that** (**oti**) you are wretched and miserable and poor and blind and naked, ¹⁸I advise you to buy from Me gold refined by fire **so that** (**ina**) you may become rich, and white garments **so that** (**ina**) you may clothe yourself, and **that** the shame of your nakedness will not be revealed; and eye salve to anoint your eyes **so that** (**ina**) you may see.*

V. 17 shows the limits of *oti*'s diversity and v. 18 illustrates the consistency of *ina*'s telic property. The first *oti* (because) is a rare case (3% of John's uses of *oti*) of not being A *oti* B, but instead is "*oti* B A", where *oti* B is v. 17 and A is v. 18. You can see (p. 124-126) that *oti*'s "outcome A ← source B" relationship is not disturbed by reading "v. 18, v. 17", which is the normal A *oti* B sequence. No matter which verse is read first, v. 17 (*oti* B) shows why Jesus' advice in v. 18 was needed so much. The second *oti* is untranslated and its B identifies specifically what the Laodicean believers were saying. The third *oti* B identifies specifically what they did not know but should have known.

All 3 *ina*'s in v. 18 show *ina*'s source-outcome relationship (the NAS inserted "that" [I boldfaced it] from the second *ina* to help English readers). Buying from Jesus gold refined by fire would produce the outcome of being truly rich. Buying from Him white garments would produce clothing oneself and not revealing the shame of being naked. Buying from Him eye salve to anoint one's eyes would produce the outcome of seeing rightly. All 3 are unlike the "current facts" in v. 17.

This side-by-side comparison of John's use of *ina* and *oti* provides 52 *ina*'s (almost ¼ of John's 213 *ina*'s) and 53 *oti*'s in 45 contexts. I find that John was totally consistent to use *oti* with its two meanings (B identifies A in 42, B shows why A in 16 [5 mean both]) that differ from a telic *ina*. I also find (again) that all 52 *ina's* can be telic and that no *ina* must identify an antecedent in A like *oti* does, despite the usual assumption in translating John.

This data adds to the huge loss of content we saw from assuming that John sometimes used *ina* to act like *oti* (Chapters 1-7). In Chapter 8 we can see that this assumption is not needed: every *ina* out of 213 *ina's* has a reasonable telic meaning. In this Apx. 3 we see that John was extremely careful and consistent in his use of *ina* and *oti*.

I find that assuming John used *ina* as if it were *oti* is not consistent with the facts of his usage, and so I conclude that this assumption is wrong and veils important truth.

Comparing John's Use of Ina and Oti After Every Legō

John's careful and consistent distinction of *ina* from *oti* can help you "know" that he would not write *ina* as if it were *oti* in crucially important SIV's. John consistently used *oti* with its two meanings after certain verbs, and *ina* with its telic meaning after mostly different verbs. An exception is *legō* (say, …). John used *legō ina* 3 times and *legō oti* 53 times (like some of my Greek sources, I put *epō* [*eipon*…] under *legō*). In this section I start with three 1John 1 verses, then discuss all 3 "*legō ina*" verses, then list all 53 "*legō oti*" verses, and finally show 4 *legō oti* examples that provide further insights and confirmation.

1John 1:6: *If we say that [oti] we have fellowship with Him* [end of B] *and yet walk in the darkness* [end of the contingent "if" statement and its subjunctive], *we lie and do not practice the truth.* "B" in v. 6, 8, and 10 identifies (specifies) what we could say (the "if" in v. 6, 8, 10 causes my contingent "could say"). And B in each of these verses is a lie and not an outcome of what we say (as *ina* would have shown).

1John 1:8: *If we say that [oti] we have no sin* [end of B], *we are deceiving ourselves and the truth is not in us.*

1John 1:10: *If we* say *that* [*oti*] *we have not sinned* [end of B]*, we make Him a liar and His word is not in us.*

John 11:41-42: [41]*...Then Jesus raised His eyes, and said, "Father, I thank You that You have heard Me.* [42]*I knew that You always hear Me; but because of the people standing around I* said *it,* [b]*so that* [*ina*] *they* may believe *that You sent Me."* The content and context make it clear: Jesus said *"Father, I thank You that You have heard Me"* in v. 41 with a desired outcome stated after *ina*: *"they may believe that You sent Me."*

John 13:29: *For some were* supposing*, because Judas had the money box, that* [*oti*] *Jesus was* saying *to him, "Buy the things we have need of for the feast"; or else,* *that* [*ina*] *he should give something to the poor.* *Oti*'s A is supposing, and its B is v. 29 after *oti* and identifies two specific things some supposed. A telic *ina* shows one supposed thing: Jesus said His statement to Judas to produce its outcome: he gives that amount to the poor. V. 29 does not show the disciples' supposing that Jesus told Judas, "Give something to...". The Bible never shows that Jesus told a disciple, "give something" or "just do something", but He said the specific thing to be given or done. Some disciples would not suppose Jesus said to Judas, "You *'should give* something*...'".*

1John 5:16: [a]*If anyone sees his brother committing a sin not leading to death, he shall ask and God will for him give life to those who commit sin not leading to death.* [b]*There is a sin leading to death; I do not* say *that* [*ina*] *he should make request for this.* As we saw (p. 47), John did not say v. 16a to cause this bad outcome: v. 16b's presumptive asking. In v. 16b John is still emphasizing asking God according to His will (v. 14-16a, whose *aiteō* for "ask" 4 times is a humbler word than *erōtaō* in v. 16b: p. 47). And so we see that all 3 *legō ina* B's do not identify A.

All 53 *legō oti*'s: John 1:32; 1:50; 3:11; 4:17; 4:20; 4:35; 4:42; 4:51; 4:52; 5:15; 5:24; 5:25; 6:14; 6:36; 6:42; 7:12; 7:42; 8:24; 8:33; 8:34; 8:48; 8:54; 8:55; 9:9,9; 9:11; 9:17; 9:19; 9:23; 9:41; 10:7; 10:36; 10:41; 11:40; 12:34; 13:11; 13:21; 13:33; 16:15; 16:20; 16:26; 18:8; 18:9; 18:37; 20:13; 21:23.   1John 1:6; 1:8; 1:10; 2:4; 4:20.   Rev. 3:17; 18:7.

John 3:11: *Truly, truly, I* say *to you,* [*oti*] *we speak of what we know and testify of what we have seen, and you do not accept our testimony.* *Oti* is an untranslated word after "Truly, truly, I say to you", and its B (v. 11 after *oti*) identifies what He was about to say (*oti*'s A). John used 7 *oti*'s, 18 no word, and 0 *ina*'s in Jesus' 25 "Truly, truly, I say to you, '...'" (... is a direct quote).

John 4:51: *As he was now going down, his slaves met him,* <u>*saying*</u> ***that*** *[oti] his son was living.* "His son was living" <u>identified</u> <u>what they said</u> and <u>definitely was not an outcome</u> of what they said: his son's living came before their report of it.

John 13:10b-11: *..."you are clean, but not all of you."* [11]*For He knew the one who was betraying Him; for this reason He* <u>*said*</u>, *"[oti] Not all of you are clean."* Oti is <u>not translated</u> except for quotation marks (a comma in the KJV), which clearly shows *oti*'s meaning: to <u>IDENTIFY SPECIFICALLY</u> what was said. Of 53 *legō oti*'s, 33 <u>quote something</u> <u>with</u> *oti* <u>not translated</u> (as in 13:11), but John <u>never</u> used *ina* to quote something. 33 *oti*'s to 0 *ina*'s shows <u>consistency</u>.

John 16:14b-15: *... He will take of Mine and will disclose it to you.* [15]*All things that the Father has are Mine; therefore I* <u>*said*</u> ***that*** *[oti] He takes of Mine and will disclose it to you.* You can easily see that the B after *oti* <u>identified</u> what Jesus said, but here we can see more. Jesus quote in v. 15 of Himself in v. 14 changed the tense of "take" without changing the content of the quote. John 13:10-11 (the previous example) makes a slightly larger rewording in the pair of statements there. Both examples illustrate the precise meaning of "say [*legō*] *oti*": in <u>identifying what was said</u>, a quote keeps the true content but may not be all words exactly as was said.

In conclusion, in John's 53 times when *oti* followed *legō*, *legō oti* B identified A (what was said) 51 or 52 times, the exceptions being John 9:17a (*legō oti*=because) and either *oti* meaning in John 20:13. John also used *legō ina* 3 times, but always as a telic-*ina*: no *legō ina* B identified what was said. <u>IF</u> John did use *ina* to <u>identify like *oti*</u>, then we could expect him to use about 24 *legō ina* B's when he identifies A [$213/(213+234) \times 51$ (or 52) = 24 *ina*'s]. John's actual use of <u>0 *ina* B's</u> and <u>51 or 52 *oti* B's</u> to identify A is a <u>decisive distinction</u> in his use of *ina* and *oti*. The final 4 examples (above) show two more whole groups to see how differently John consistently treated *oti* and *ina* with *legō*.

A Stark Contrast: Ina's Contingent Subjunctive B-Verb Vs.
Oti's Indicative B-Verb in John 11-17

This section provides the detailed report on <u>every</u> *ina* and *oti* in John 11-17 (all 75 *ina*'s and 94 *oti*'s in John 11-17, a sample where I do not select which *ina*'s and *oti*'s to consider). We first see John's consistently indicative-verb after *oti*, and then see how each and every B-verb after *ina* can be subjunctive.

On p. 110 I reported that *oti*'s B-verb is consistently indicative, and the only subjunctive *oti*-B-verb (John 11:56) is contained in a question emphasizing that a person's answer was contingent. Here I locate the 94 *oti*'s, and then discuss the only 3 complications I see to a clearly consistent indicative *oti*-B-verb (the 3 are underlined-bold in the list):

John 11: 6 9 10 13 15 20 22 24 27 31 31 40 41 42 42 47 50 51 **56**
John 12: 6 6 9 11 12 16 18 19 34 34 39 41 49 50
John 13: 1 3 3 11 19 21 29 33 35
John 14: 2 10 **11** 12 17 17 19 **20** 22 28 28 28 31
John 15: 5 15 15 18 19 21 25 27
John 16: 3 4 4 6 9 10 11 14 15 17 19 19 20 21 21 26 27 27 30 30 32
John 17: 7 8 8 8 9 14 21 23 24 25

B-verbs for 91 of the 94 *oti*'s in John 11-17 are indicative, and I see no need to explain. The 1 subjunctive in John 11:56 and the 2 "no-B-verbs" do NOT disturb *oti*'s 100% indicative (factual), but need to be explained. In John 11:56 people were asking each other's opinions: *"What do you think; that [**oti**] He will not come [elthē] to the feast at all?"* Perschbacher shows that *elthē* is subjunctive. This makes sense from the question: their opinion about its answer was contingent, having nothing to do with the future fact of His showing up or not. Therefore the contingency implied in the question itself caused the subjunctive – *oti* did not cause it.

The final 2 *oti*'s are in John 14:11 and 14:20, which have no explicit verb in *oti* B. The solution is in 14:10, where Jesus asks: *"Do you not believe that [**oti**] I am in the Father* ["am" is not in Greek, but is well-inserted in every translation I find], *and the Father is [estin, present* indicative] *in Me?" Oti* B of v. 10 is repeated in v. 11: *"Believe Me that* [**oti**] *I am in the Father and the Father is in Me"* ("am" and "is" are not in the Greek).   Literal translators can insert v. 11's verbs from the indicative "is" in v. 10.   V. 20 repeats the *oti* B part of v. 11, also with no verbs.   Therefore in this sample of <u>all 94 *oti*'s in John 11-17</u>, <u>I find John totally consistent</u> in his use of an <u>indicative verb in *oti* B</u>.

P. 110 reports that all 75 *ina*'s can be subjunctive: in this section I identify each *ina*-B-verb from my sources of Greek. *Ina* is more important than *oti* in our examination, and also adds a complication: a few important *ina*-B-verbs have the same subjunctive as indicative and/or imperative.   Therefore for every *ina* in John 11-17, I write the transliterated word in my Greek text (with ō for omega and ē for eta) and every mood in my lexicon.   On p. 78-86, I quote each NAS verse with its B-verb underlined. I repeat my goal for Apx. 1-3: to present my case for John's purely telic *ina*, but also to not bury any relevant "complication" (here you can see some of my data).

John 11:4 *doxasthē*   subjunctive
John 11:11 *exupnisō*   subjunctive
John 11:15 *pisteusēte*   subjunctive
John 11:16 *apothanōmen*   subjunctive
John 11:19 *paramuthēsōntai*   subjunctive
John 11:31 *klausē*   subjunctive
John 11:37 *apothanē*   subjunctive
John 11:42 *pisteusōsin*   subjunctive
John 11:50 *apothanē*   subjunctive   *apolētai*   subjunctive
John 11:52 *sunagagē*   subjunctive
John 11:53 *apokteinōsin*   subjunctive
John 11:55 *agnisōsin*   subjunctive
John 11:57 *mēnusē*   subjunctive   *piasōsin*   subjunctive
John 12:7 *tērēsē*   subjunctive
John 12:9 *idōsin*   subjunctive

John 12:10 *apokteinōsin* subjunctive

John 12:20 *proskunēsōsin* subjunctive

John 12:23 *doxasthē* subjunctive

John 12:35 *katalabē* subjunctive

John 12:36 *genēsthe* subjunctive

John 12:38 *plērōthē* subjunctive

John 12:40 *idōsin* subjunctive   *noēsōsin* subjunctive
  straphōsin subjunctive

John 12:42 *genōntai* subjunctive

John 12:46 *meinē* subjunctive

John 12:47ab *krinō, sōsō* Both verbs are 1st person singular and can be subjunctive aorist or indicative. Jesus said the same truth in the 3rd person singular in John 3:17, which specifies the subjunctive.

John 13:1 *metabē* subjunctive

John 13:2 *paradoi* subjunctive

John 13:15 *poiēte* subjunctive

John 13:18 *plērōthē* subjunctive

John 13:19 *pisteuēte* subjunctive

John 13:29 *dō* subjunctive

John 13:34ab *agapate* subjunctive indicative imperative (all 2nd person plural, present tense, active)

John 14:3 *ēte* subjunctive (present tense: the imperfect indicative with its continued past action is inconsistent with Jesus' statement)

John 14:13 *doxasthē* subjunctive

John 14:16 *ē* subjunctive

John 14:29 *pisteusēte* subjunctive

John 14:31 *gnō* subjunctive

John 15:2 *pherē* subjunctive

John 15:8 *pherēte* subjunctive

John 15:11 *ē* subjunctive   *plērōthē* subjunctive

John 15:12 *agapate* subjunctive indicative imperative (all 2nd person plural, present tense, active)

John 15:13 *thē* subjunctive

John 15:16 *upagēte* subjunctive   *pherēte*   subjunctive
  menē subjunctive

John 15:16 *dō*   subjunctive

John 15:17 *agapate*   subjunctive   indicative   imperative   (all 2nd person plural, present tense, active)

John 15:25 *plērōthē*   subjunctive

John 16:1   *skandalisthēte*   subjunctive

John 16:2   *doxē*   subjunctive

John 16:4   *mnēmoneuēte*   subjunctive

John 16:7   *apelthō*   subjunctive

John 16:24 *ē*   subjunctive

John 16:30 *erōta*   subjunctive   indicative   (both 3rd person singular, present tense, active)

John 16:32 *skorpisthēte*   subjunctive   *aphēte*   subjunctive

John 16:33 *echēte*   subjunctive

John 17:1   *doxasē*   subjunctive

John 17:2   *dōsē*   subjunctive

John 17:3   *ginōskōsin*   subjunctive

John 17:4   *poiēsō*   subjunctive aorist tense: indicative future tense is ruled out by Jesus' having finished this work

John 17:11 *ōsin*   subjunctive

John 17:12 *plērōthē*   subjunctive

John 17:13 *echōsin*   subjunctive

John 17:15 *arēs*   subjunctive

John 17:15 *tērēsēs*   subjunctive

John 17:19 *ōsin*   subjunctive

John 17:21 *ōsin*   subjunctive

John 17:21 *ōsin*   subjunctive

John 17:21 *pisteuē*   subjunctive

John 17:22 *ōsin*   subjunctive

John 17:23 *ōsin*   subjunctive

John 17:23 *ginōskē*   subjunctive

John 17:24 *ōsin*   subjunctive

John 17:24 *theōrōsin*   subjunctive

John 17:26 *ē*   subjunctive

As you can see, my Greek sources (p. 109) show that every B-verb of its *ina* in John 11-17 (75 *ina*'s) <u>can</u> be subjunctive (contingent).

Because the indicative and subjunctive of a few verbs in the list are spelled the same, those verbs could be subjunctive or something else without a further examination. A further analysis indicated in the list eliminates every non-subjunctive except *agapate* (John 13:34 twice and 15:12, 17) and *erōta* (16:30). Again, because even these two exceptions can be subjunctive, NO *INA* in John 11-17 goes against the claim that John always used a subjunctive verb in the B after *ina* in his Gospel and Epistles: this confirms the contingent nature of a telic outcome. This section's report on all 94 *oti*'s in John 11-17 (p. 142-143) adds that John consistently wrote *oti*'s B-verb in the factual indicative. This section's comparison provides another extensive demonstration of John's distinct use of *ina* and *oti*.

A Telic Ina Even in Marshall's Chosen Example in Matt. 5:29

This section is a final add-on to checking John's use of a purely telic *ina*. On p. 17 I quote Marshall about a non-telic *ina* in Matt. 5:29. Even though this is not John's use of *ina*, v. 29 was identified in the foundation of our examination, so that it could help to see that v. 29 can also have a good telic meaning for *ina*. I use telic's meaning of connecting a relevant outcome with its source: Matt. 26:58, Rom. 6:22, 2Cor. 11:15, Heb. 6:11, James 5:11, and 1Peter 1:9 are examples of this source-outcome meaning of *telos*. (In contrast, "telic" is often limited to show purpose only, but this does not fit John's use of *ina*).

Matt. 5:29: *If your right eye makes you stumble, tear it out and throw it from you; for it is better for you* **to [ina]** *lose one of the parts of your body, than for your whole body to be thrown into hell.* Source A is v. 29 before *ina*: tear out my right eye if it makes me stumble. B is the outcome described in v. 29 after *ina*: losing a part of my body by doing A is a better projected outcome than losing my whole body forever as an outcome of not doing A.

About the Author (Jim Tarter)

I met God in 1972 when I was 27, a Ph.D. physicist and an agnostic. He quickly started showing me that Jesus authentically represented God, and that the Bible was His word. I started reading the Bible thinking that it was full of contradictions, but it surprised me. The Bible's contents provided much evidence to show that the Lord had inspired and then protected these contents to say precisely what He wanted them to say.

Having missed God so completely in my life and in the world, I read the Bible with a deep hunger to learn more about this One who knew my thoughts and who numbers the hairs on each person's head. I also joined a church in Pittsburgh, PA. The pastor was Joseph Garlington, who provided a rich spiritual foundation. This congregation had many other believers who had met Jesus and sought to put His word into practice. When I moved to Roanoke, VA, in 1978, I actively participated in another congregation that was "alive in Jesus". Such experiences helped me to learn more about God and His ways, and have provided many perspectives about His calling for the Church in the Bible, what we have done in reality, and what we need to do to fulfill His word concerning us.

I am an elder at Grace Covenant Church in Roanoke and taught in public schools in 1976-2009. I wrote two books in the 1990s: *God's Word to the United States* (especially from Obadiah) and *Why, God?* (from the book of Job). Updates of both books plus 22 other books about the Bible are available at www.lulu.com (see below).

In summers my wife Nita and I have taken extensive trips to South Sudan, the Congo, and elsewhere. Her heart for Jesus and sensitivity to His leadings have blessed me mightily and equipped me to go further into my life in Christ Jesus.

Years after I first met God through Jesus, He started opening up whole books of the Bible, which provide life-giving perspectives that the vast majority of the Church has not yet appreciated. This book can help us confirm God's calling and provision for our life in Jesus that John's Gospel and 1John show but few can see now.

As I write this, my books are available at www.lulu.com as a paperback, a PDF ebook, and an epub ebook for digital devices. Typing "James Tarter" in the search space at the top will take you to my books. A PDF contains the whole book and is free at Lulu (you may arrange my books in order of ascending price). If you find the $2.99 ebook, look further for the free PDF.